W9-AUN-948

KEEP MOVING

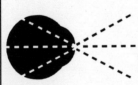

This Large Print Book carries the
Seal of Approval of N.A.V.H.

KEEP MOVING

AND OTHER TIPS AND TRUTHS ABOUT AGING

DICK VAN DYKE
WITH TODD GOLD

THORNDIKE PRESS

A part of Gale, Cengage Learning

GALE
CENGAGE Learning®

Farmington Hills, Mich • San Francisco • New York • Waterville, Maine
Meriden, Conn • Mason, Ohio • Chicago

GALE
CENGAGE Learning

LIBRARY OF CONGRESS CATALOGING-IN-PUBLICATION DATA

Names: Van Dyke, Dick, author. | Gold, Todd author.
Title: Keep moving, and other tips and truths about aging / by Dick Van Dyke with Todd Gold.
Description: Large print edition. | Waterville, Maine : Thorndike Press, a part of Gale, Cengage Learning, 2016. | © 2015 | Series: Thorndike Press large print biographies and memoirs
Identifiers: LCCN 2015042216| ISBN 9781410487421 (hardcover) | ISBN 1410487423 (hardcover)
Subjects: LCSH: Van Dyke, Dick. | Television actors and actresses—United States—Biography. | Comedians—United States—Biography. | Aging—Anecdotes. | Old age—Anecdotes. | Large type books.
Classification: LCC PN2287.V335 A3 2016 | DDC 791.4302/8092—dc23
LC record available at http://lccn.loc.gov/2015042216

Published in 2016 by arrangement with Weinstein Books, a member of the Perseus Books Group

I dedicate this book to
my beautiful wife, Arlene,
who was invaluable in editing this tome.
Not to mention keeping me fit as a
fiddle and younger than springtime.

CONTENTS

INTRODUCTION

In 1979 the great filmmaker Orson Welles appeared in a television commercial for Paul Masson wines. The thirty-second spot opened with him turning down the music on his stereo. "It took Beethoven four years to write that symphony," he said in his memorable *bosso profondo* voice. "Some things can't be rushed. Good music. And good wine."

In a 2015 update I would like to add something else to that list.

Old age.

Old age should be revered, admired, respected, treated to dinner, opened and allowed to breathe like a fine wine, given aisle seats on an airplane, helped up the stairs, and looked upon with patience, especially in the checkout line at the grocery store. Old people like to make conversation with the checkers. If approached correctly, says this former Boy Scout, old age should be considered a merit badge for a life well lived. Old age should be a lot of things. But it should not be rushed.

I know from experience.

I was pronounced old way before my time.

I was working on the movie *Chitty Chitty Bang Bang* in England and suffered an injury while shooting the musical number "Toot Sweets." If you recall, it was an elaborate production number set in a confectionary kitchen that celebrated the invention of a revolutionary new candy, the toot sweet. Before the scene I did not take the time to warm up (I never warmed up back then), and in the part of the dance where we spin around on bakery carts in a mix of ballet and acrobatics, I felt the muscle in the back of my left leg pop, like a rubber band that snaps and loses its elasticity. Then, oh boy, did it start to hurt!

I sloughed it off, of course — or tried to. I told myself it was a simple muscle pull and that, in the spirit of show business, the scene must continue. But when the pain not only persisted but grew worse, to the point where I could not pretend to walk normally or limp with a covert abnormality, I feared the damage might be more severe.

What did I know? I had never been injured before. I took a few days off and rested my leg, but the throbbing continued. Someone on the crew found me a doctor. I'm not a fan of doctor visits for anything more than regular maintenance — my annual check under the hood — but I knew I had to see a professional about this injury.

The doctor saw me right away and took X-rays. A short time later he delivered a startling diagnosis: severe arthritis.

"My God," he said, tapping his finger against the X-ray and shaking his head gravely, "you're covered with arthritis from head to foot. I'm surprised you could dance. I've never seen so much arthritis in a single person."

"What about a married person?" I hoped a joke might lighten the seriousness of his delivery. It didn't.

"Married or single, you're literally suffused with arthritis," he said.

"What about the pain in my leg?" I asked.

"It's the arthritis."

This was not a joking matter, he explained. The condition was serious, far worse than a muscle tear, and it was only going to get worse.

"Within five to seven years you will be using a walker, if not in a wheelchair," he said.

A walker? A wheelchair?

Those words upended my relationship to

the world. My center of gravity, like every-body else, was under my own two feet, and I was being told those two feet of mine were about to be rendered lame, if not useless. The prognosis scared me to death, to the point where I did something rash, some-thing downright defiant. I stood up in the examining room, then and there, and I started to move. Not just move — I lit into a dance, as if proving to myself I could still order my body to do a soft shoe anytime I wanted, despite the pain in my leg. The doc-tor was astonished.

"My God!" he said as if watching a dead man start to breathe again.

My God, indeed.

That was in 1967. I was forty years old. And I have not stopped moving ever since.

Nor do I plan to hit the stop button anytime soon. I am 89 years old as I write this at my home in Malibu, California, which means I am in my 90th year on this planet, and by definition, I am old. Very old, I suppose — older than the average male, who now lives to be 76.4 years old (the aver-age female lives to be 81.2). But if you are 65 or thereabouts today, your life expec-tancy is even longer. You should start think-ing of 65 as the new 40. In other words, you aren't old yet — you are merely on the launching pad of old age.

I never considered myself old until I was asked to share my tips and thoughts on old age here. I don't act old, and I don't feel it. I don't think like an old person, whatever that means. But according to Wikipedia, old age "consists of ages nearing or surpassing the life expectancy of human beings, and thus the end of the human life cycle." If you keep reading that definition, it includes susceptibility to disease, limited ability to bounce back from illness, increased frailty, memory loss, loneliness . . . and so on. It does not paint a rosy picture.

I'm not going to deny the harsh realities of living a long life, because I have experienced my share of them. But there is a flip-side to old age, and as a card-carrying the-glass-is-half-full optimist, I am going to unfurl the gray flag, wave it proudly, and declare that getting old doesn't have to be a dreary weather report.

In 99.9 percent of the stories I have heard it is better than the alternative, if only because you get to see what happens next.

How can you not be curious?

One of the things you realize when looking back across the decades is that we all have a front-row seat to what Thomas Jefferson called "the course of human events." If there's a better show in town, I have yet to hear about it in my long lifetime — and neither has anyone else. It is *the* show.

With Baby Boomers swelling the ranks of AARP and asking without embarrassment for their senior citizen discounts at the movie theater, and with people turning sixty-five expected to live on average well into their eighties, more of us (no, make that more of you — I'm already there) than at any time in human history are going to start the day staring at our reflection in the bathroom mirror and asking the same question I have asked myself many times: Who's that old person looking at me?

In this book I am going to tell you that the person with gray or thinning hair, wrinkles, dark spots, sagging skin, a slight stoop, cloudy vision and ears that may need fine tuning is you. But I am also going to tell you the truth about this new normal, formally known as geezer-dom: you don't have to act your age. You don't even have to feel it. And if it does attempt to elbow its way into your life, you do not have to pay attention.

If I am out shopping and hear music playing in a store, I start to dance. If I want to sing, I sing. I read books and get excited about new ideas. I enjoy myself. I don't think about the way I am supposed to act at my age — or at any age. As far as I know, there is no manual for old age. There is no test you have to pass. There is no way you have to behave. There is no such thing as "age appropriate."

On the following pages you will find my tips and truths about life as your hair grays, your knees wear out, you need glasses to find your glasses, and you ask, "How the hell did this happen to me?" You will also find me discussing the realities we all face as we confront the fact that the majority of our days are behind us — though, as I can attest, that is not meant to imply the best days are also in the rearview mirror.

As you will discover, I try to keep things simple. A friend of mine once said, "Just a spoonful of sugar helps the medicine go down." She was right. When people ask my secret to staying youthful at an age when getting up and down from your chair on your own is considered an accomplishment, you know what I tell them?

"Keep moving."

One more thing: old age is not a death sentence. It's a stage of life. And . . . and . . . I forgot what I was going to say.

That happens too. . . .

Eventually you will reach a point
where you will stop lying about your
age and start bragging about it.
— **WILL ROGERS**

Every morning, I wake up and read
the obituaries —
and if I'm not in them, I have breakfast.
— **CARL REINER**

PLAYING WITH HOUSE MONEY

There are many different ways to celebrate turning eighty-nine. On December 12, 2014, the night before my birthday, I was in the audience at the Malibu Civic Theater watching my wife, Arlene, belly dance. She'd been taking classes at Melanie Kareem's Middle Eastern Dance School for a few years and was performing a solo in their end-of-the-year recital. She looked gorgeous in a silver top and black skirt that shimmered with every shake of her hips. I was mesmerized.

After about three minutes I couldn't sit still anymore. Arlene had cast a spell over me, and there in my seat, my body began to mimic Arlene's movements and move to the rhythmic Egyptian music until suddenly I was on my feet and heading toward the stage.

I did not want to detract from her big moment in the spotlight, but I couldn't help myself. I had spent six decades on the stage, on top of which I had practiced moves with her at home, and I saw no reason to stop what came naturally, even if I was entering my last year as an octogenarian. Why sit on the sidelines of life at any age, especially at mine?

I didn't. Standing beside Arlene, I shimmied and shook, my hips going right and then left, my arms and wrists undulating like long snakes. All of our rehearsing at home paid off, as we looked in sync, though I added my own solo on the side of the stage, a final series of bumps and shakes in my blue jeans, before relinquishing the stage again to my beautiful wife.

"You were great," someone said to me afterward. "It's amazing. You don't act your age at all."

Amazing? Why is it amazing that I don't act my age? Why should I act my age? Or more to the point, how is someone my age supposed to act? Old age is part fact, part state of mind, part luck, and wholly something best left for other people to ponder, not you or me. Why waste the time? I don't.

The following night — my actual birthday, December 13 — we were out again. We went to a holiday party at the home of our friends Frank and Fay Mancuso. They throw first-class parties, and this one was no exception. Christmas carolers in Dickens-style outfits stood by the door and greeted guests with a buoyant version of the seasonal hymn "Hark, the Herald Angels Sing," but they segued seamlessly to "Happy Birthday" as soon as Arlene and I came up the front walk. My wife had tipped off the hosts, despite my preference against such attention. But their harmonizing was perfect, absolutely gorgeous, and there is no bigger fan of four-part harmony than me. I stood there, beaming.

"Do you take requests?" I asked.

"Sure," one of them said as the others nodded.

"Do you know 'Caroling, Caroling'? I love the Nat King Cole version, and for some reason I never hear it on the radio during the holidays."

They knew the classic holiday song, of course, and as their voices wove together in beautiful harmony, I stepped away from Arlene's side and joined them. "Ding-dong, ding-dong," we sang, "Christmas bells are ringing . . ." If I had worn a Victorian-era suit, I might have sung with them all night.

Inside, the house had been turned into a winter wonderland, starting with a tree in the entry that was at least twenty feet tall, if not taller, and decorated with such an abundance of ornaments and lights that I jokingly said to Arlene, "You could break your neck trying to see the star at the top."

In the dining room we encountered an actual light snowfall, a unique backdrop to a delicious Italian feast that also included a sixteen-piece orchestra playing holiday classics and standards — in other words, my favorites. Then Mr. and Mrs. Santa Claus passed out fancy caramel-covered apples and brought out an enormous cake full of candles. It was one way to say hello to my ninetieth year.

Ironically, I hadn't planned to do anything for my birthday. I had given the okay to my wife to organize a big party the next year, my ninetieth, but my intention was to sit this one out. I don't need a party every year. I am fine with celebrating the big ones, the birthdays ending in a five or a zero. Otherwise I don't like the fuss or attention. I am most comfortable with a simple dinner and visits or calls from my four children, seven grandchildren, and growing list of great-grandchildren.

I think birthday parties are best for kids. They are learning to count. Let them practice. At my age I don't need the practice. Or the boredom. If I started to count, I would lose interest before I reached fifteen. I would never make it into the fifties, let alone the eighties. So what's the point?

However, I do like cake. My mother baked a birthday cake for me every year, an angel food cake with chocolate frosting. To this day it is still my favorite flavor. She sent me one when I was in the Air Force. It did not travel well through the mail and arrived in a pile of crumbs. I did not care. My buddies and I stuck a candle in it and ate every morsel.

From what I have observed, birthdays get scary as you march through your twenties. At thirty, you don't know whether to celebrate: what's to get excited about — the end of youth? The beginning of adulthood? I overheard someone say that fifty is the new thirty. Does that make thirty the new ten? On the *Today Show* recently one of the anchors declared that sixty is the new forty — and that was part of a week-long showcase of experts telling people how to live to be a hundred. What's the point here — is it to stay young or live to be old? Or both?

More people than ever before are crossing the line into senior citizenship, and I see them being intensely curious about how to make it work, how to do it better than their parents or grandparents. These are Baby

Boomers, the generation who once screamed, "Hope I die before I get old." That line should be rewritten, "Hope I die before I *feel* old." That is the crux of the matter.

Except for a three- to four-month period, which I will go into later, I have never felt old. When I turned fifty, typically the point when people think they're beginning to head downhill, I was in fine fettle mentally and physically, and my fettle got even finer when I starred in a traveling production of *Music Man.* I toured the country for a year — a new city every week. When it finished, I was fifty-one and in the best shape of my life. I returned to the ranch my first wife, Margie, and I owned in the Arizona desert and realized I couldn't stay there and do nothing — which was what Margie loved about that place. It was the beginning of the end of our marriage.

At sixty-five, I was halfway into a thirty-plus-year relationship with a new mate, Michelle Triola, a woman with an immense appetite for treating life as a party — and when there wasn't a party, she organized one. We enjoyed life together. We traveled and sailed, and I had no plans of doing much other than spending my senior years in a leisurely pursuit of adventure. Then producer Fred Silverman wanted to do a spinoff of William Conrad's series *Jake and the Fatman,* and he wanted me in the lead role. "You'll play a surgeon who solves crimes," he said.

I agreed to one episode. As I said, I was in pursuit of fun and leisure. I thought that would be my full-time job. After the episode aired, though, Freddie said the network wanted to order an hour-long series based on my character. It was called *Diagnosis Murder.* I said, "Freddie, I'm sixty-five years old. I can't do an hour series."

He said do one. Then he said do another. And so on. That went on for ten years. I was seventy-five when I finally said "enough."

But slowing down was not on the agenda. That same year I started an a cappella singing group, the Vantastix, and we booked shows across the country, at any place that would have us. We still perform together. Singing is my retirement. Others play golf — and that's fine. I may even take it up one day when I get old.

That may not happen. My mother, a beautiful woman in her younger days and regal looking as she aged, lived until she was ninety-six. As a kid, I would have long conversations with her as she did the dishes, while my father barely talked to me at all. He said even less to my brother, Jerry. Before getting married, Dad had been a bon vivant around town — without money. He played the clarinet and saxophone in a band, had played semipro baseball, and once won a left-handed golf tournament. A jack-of-all-talents. Then I came along, and he stopped that life. He became a traveling salesman, which he hated. It made him angry about his fate. He was tall, thin, and wiry like me and genetically poised to live a long life, and he likely would have if he hadn't been a chain-smoker. He died at seventy-six of emphysema.

His father — my Grandfather Van Dyke — was my real mentor. He filled in while my father was on the road, and in many other ways. He worked in the shop at the railroad and had massive, muscular forearms as proof of all the pounding and lifting he did on that large equipment. Until Charles Atlas came along with his enormous chest and biceps, the mark of a strong man was big forearms (think Popeye). My grandfather was cut from that mold. He died at age fifty-six from a ruptured aneurysm. He went instantly.

His wife — my grandmother — continued to live in the family's house with his mother, my great-grandmother, who passed away in her eighties, leaving my grandmother on her own for the first time in her life. She was the proverbial small-town, provincial Midwesterner. She had never traveled outside of our hometown, Danville, Illinois, and never ventured, as far as I knew, beyond the daily routines that filled her days. She knew her neighbors, but as they began to pass away, she had less to do and fewer people to talk to. I worried that the isolation of living alone would drive her to a premature grave. I put her in a nearby rest home.

Though it was nice, I was unsure whether she would take to the communal surroundings. But not only did she take to it, she took over. She ran the kitchen. She got involved in everyone's business. She was full of stories. One day she called me up and said, "Dickie, I didn't know that people were the way they are."

She was in her late eighties when *Mary Poppins* was released in theaters, and she got to see it. They had a premiere in our hometown. During the screening she said, "I always knew Dickie was built like a racehorse."

One day I visited her at the rest home. She was sitting on her bed when I came into her room. Ordinarily she liked to hear me

27

tell stories about Carl Reiner, her favorite from *Your Show of Shows* and my boss on *The Dick Van Dyke Show,* but this particular time she took charge of the conversation.

"I have some snapshots you've never seen," she said. Excited, she reached behind her to get the pictures. Somehow she did a complete backward somersault in the bed. If you thought the little stumble I did over the ottoman at the start of *The Dick Van Dyke Show* was something, you should have seen this. Even more impressive, she somersaulted forward again, with barely a pause in her conversation, as if it were nothing out of the ordinary.

But that was my grandmother. She was lighthearted — never worried about much of anything.

I inherited her sense of humor and ease and maybe also her ability to take a tumble and bounce back up with a smile. Though unlike her, as a younger man I was a worrier. As a nightclub performer and then TV host, I worried about how I was going to support my wife and young children. I mention that frequently and am sure you will find me talking about it again because I did not have much ambition or secure employment. And yet things worked out: I still marvel at my good luck.

Today I don't worry about anything. At eighty-nine, what's the point? But I don't think worrying served much of a purpose when I was younger. It was a waste of time, I suppose. It was an attitude suppressor. The less you worry, the better your attitude is, and a positive, worry-free, guilt-free attitude is key to enjoying life at any age — especially old age. A thousand years ago people didn't live long enough to worry about anything other than finding their next meal and avoiding becoming some ravenous beast's next meal. If people did manage to live a long time, their family or tribe took care of them. Very often they worshipped them, the wise elders of the clan.

I can see heads nodding: if only that were the case today.

It is a relatively recent phenomenon that human beings worry about old age, Social Security, medical bills, and long-term care. But you can only plan so much. In general, things either work out or they don't, and if they don't, you figure out something else, a plan B. There's nothing wrong with plan B. Most of life, as I have learned, is a plan B. Or a plan C. Or plans L, M, N, O, P.

Here is the truth: your teens and twenties are your plan A. At fifty, you're assessing whether plan B or plan C or any of the other plans you hatched actually worked. Your sixties and seventies are an improvisation. There is no blueprint, and quite honestly you spend a lot of time feeling grateful you're still here. Call it fate, luck, or whatever. If you make it past then, as I have, you discover a truth and joy that you wish you had known earlier: there is no plan.

As you get older, you figure this out. You relax. You exhale. You quit worrying. You shake your head with an accepting disbelief as family members and friends disappear like photos in a yearbook, leaving empty spaces where there used to be familiar faces, and occasionally you wonder when it will be your turn and what that will be like. You go for a walk — not to get from point A to point B but just because you want to feel the warm sun on your skin and enjoy fresh air. You open your eyes in the morning with surprise and delight that you're still here. You realize you're playing with house money. You are ahead of the game. You eat whatever you want. You do what you like. You smile at strangers. You wave, "Have a nice day."

And if you don't do that stuff, you should.

This will tell you a lot about me: I do the *New York Times* crossword puzzle in pen. There are three types of people: those who don't do the crossword puzzle, those who do it in pencil, and those who do it in pen. I have done the *Times*'s crossword puzzles for decades, so you would think I'd be pretty adept at them by now. But no, my ability has stayed the same over all these years. I get through Monday, Tuesday, and Wednesday pretty easily. Thursday is a test. Friday takes a while; I might carry it around with me most of the day. And if I get halfway through Saturday's puzzle, I feel pretty good about myself.

My simple pleasures. I drive a Jaguar. I eat raisin bran with blueberries in the morning and a hamburger for lunch when the craving hits. I like cookies and cake and a big bowl of ice cream every night. I asked my doctor whether I'm eating too much sugar. He said, "Dick, you're nearly ninety. Enjoy yourself."

So I do.

Age is something you do not think about until it happens, and I am here to inform you it happens slowly, with a sneaky tap on the shoulder. One day, in my seventies, I was playing volleyball at the beach, as I had for years, and I realized I was winded. That had never happened before — that was the shoulder tap. Then tennis got to be too much — another tap.

31

The thing that really got me, though, was when I had to give up sailing. I had always sailed. I loved flying across the water with the wind filling the sails. It was thrilling and always so beautiful to look across the water, with the coast in the distance and the sky overhead. It was of the moment, and I felt completely alive and in tune with the world. Then one day the boat heeled, I got disoriented, and it scared me to death. It turned out to be my inner ear — tap, tap, tap.

"You're getting old," my doctor said.

"No, I'm not," I replied. "My inner ear is not what it used to be. But I'm fine."

Both of us were right. I cultivated new hobbies. I kept moving. The only way to deal with these shoulder taps from Father Time is to accept them, deal with them, and make adjustments. As we get older, none of us stays entirely the same — and who wants to? That's what I don't understand about plastic surgery. All that nipping and tucking doesn't make you look younger — only stranger. My advice? Let the outside sag and wrinkle; change what's on the inside.

I once considered plastic surgery, though. On the first day of production on *Chitty Chitty Bang Bang* I was sitting in the makeup chair and overheard the director whisper to the makeup guy, "What are we going to do about his hooter?"

The makeup guy replied, "I'm not a plastic surgeon."

I knew I had a big nose. I was teased about it all through high school. The teacher would ask, "Does anybody know the answer to this?" From all corners of the room arose a chorus of "Dick nose."

After *Chitty Chitty Bang Bang* wrapped, I returned home to Los Angeles from England and saw a plastic surgeon. "Why are you here?" he asked.

I told him what had been said about my nose on the movie set. "It seems I need a hooter-plasty," I explained, trying to make light of a sensitive subject.

"Go home," the doctor said. "You're established. You can't do anything about it. That's who you are."

And that's the way I stayed.

Accepting that life is a perfectly imperfect experience is a crucial part of appreciating senior citizenship and coming to terms with the past. Every once in a while I will be flipping through the TV channels and see myself in a TV show or movie that I didn't think was very good when I was making it back in the sixties or seventies. Seeing it all these years later, I think, *Hey, that wasn't bad. In fact, it was pretty good.*

As a younger man, though, I lacked confidence, the confidence that comes with experience. I worried and stressed way more than I should have. Now I see that worrying and stressing never helped accomplish anything. It was only when I let myself go and had fun that the magic happened — and continues to happen.

Here's another example, this one more recent and personal. My wife is forty-six years younger than me — yes, I know the reaction people have hearing that for the first time (or the third time) — and for that reason I couldn't wait for her to turn forty. For whatever reason I thought forty sounded much more reasonable than thirty-nine — that is, until I realized no one cared about the difference in our ages as long as we were happy. We went to events together, saw friends at restaurants, all that stuff couples do, and all anyone said to me was, "Dick, it's nice to see you so happy."

We had a fantastic time celebrating her fortieth, a *Love Boat*–themed party we had on a four-story boat. Guests were asked to dress as a favorite TV character or personality from the seventies and eighties (we had a couple of Mr. Ts, a Sonny and Cher, and a handful of Magnum P.I.s). I was Mr. Roarke from *Fantasy Island,* and Arlene dressed up as Dolly Parton and kicked off the night with a spirited lip-synced rendition of "9 to 5." I morphed from Mr. Roarke into Kenny Rogers (I removed my tie and opened my shirt — I already had a white beard) and joined her in lip-syncing the Dolly Parton–Kenny Rogers hit "Islands in the Stream." The Vantastix closed the evening with a medley of songs from *Mary Poppins* and *Chitty Chitty Bang Bang.* It was my kind of birthday party — focused on someone else and total fun.

The next day I asked Arlene whether she felt any older. "No," she said. "If anything, I feel happier." Perfect. Mission accomplished.

Likewise, on the morning after my eighty-ninth birthday I opened my eyes and said to myself, "My God, this is the first day of my ninetieth year. I feel great." I got out of bed and went to the gym, where I walked on the treadmill and lifted weights, as is my daily routine. On my way home I stopped at the market, where the gang there was waiting with a present: a pound of coffee and a freshly brewed cup with a large "D" written on the side. My favorite checker, Debbie, sang "Happy Birthday."

At some point later in the day I realized that at eighty-nine, I was the same age as the stodgy old banker I had played in *Mary Poppins,* Mr. Dawes. I loved playing old people. To this day many fans of the movie don't realize that was me beneath all that makeup, stooped over, with a mop of white hair, a long beard, a curmudgeonly frown, and legs so weak I tottered precariously on a cane while singing "Fidelity Fiduciary Bank." I had pitched the idea to Walt Disney, who made me audition for the part.

I laughed as I recalled that role. Then I laughed harder, thinking about how I didn't have to pretend anymore. I *am* that old!

But getting old, I am delighted to report, is not a prescription for acting old. Consider: a few weeks after my birthday I stopped at the vitamin store to get my wife a green protein shake, as I do every day. Outside the store three students from nearby Pepperdine University were singing. One of them had a ukulele. I wandered over and started harmonizing. I didn't introduce myself; I just joined in and assumed their smiles were an invitation to keep going. We sang a handful of songs together and all had a wonderful start to the day.

Ironically, as I look ahead to my ninth — or is it my tenth? — decade, my only real concern is that I have term life insurance. It's good up until age ninety-five. If I live beyond then, it cuts off, and there's no payout. I didn't realize this when I took out the insurance fifty years ago. Who figures they'll live to be ninety-five? However, given my health and my attitude, my doctor says that I will likely live to see ninety-five and beyond. My wife says the same thing. So do my children, grandchildren, and great-grandchildren. No one expects me to go anywhere soon.

Good for me. I am not about to complain. In terms of money, though, my family will be up the creek. I probably shouldn't say this, but I may have to fake my own death before I'm ninety-five. I feel too good.

The Kid Stays in the Game

There used to be a regular poker game at Barbara Sinatra's house in Malibu, and a great group of people showed up, including Jack Lemmon, Larry Gelbart, and Gregory Peck, who wore a little green visor like an old-time gambler. Everyone was about the same age, in their late sixties or seventies. I took my longtime companion, Michelle Triola, there because she loved to play poker. One night, back when I was doing *Diagnosis Murder,* I let her off and told the gang I was going back home.

"I'm the only one here who doesn't play poker," I said.

"You're the only one here who's working," said Gregory Peck.

Oh Brother,
How Old Art Thou?

(OR, HOW DO YOU KNOW
WHEN YOU'RE OLD?)

How do you know when you're old?

People worry about this. They think about it, they plan for it, and then one day they wake up surprised. They look in the mirror and ask, "Is that really me? Am I old? How did *that* happen?" I have done that many times, though I try not to, despite the daily onslaught of insurance solicitations that arrive in the mail and the TV commercials we all see targeting the ailments, afflictions, and anxieties prevalent among us soldiers in the gray-haired army. Maybe you know you're old when you start paying attention to those commercials. I change the channel.

I have managed to avoid the question, even though all of the major birthdays that trigger such existential inquiry are in my past. I have also managed to avoid the question even though my oldest child, Chris, is sixty-five, my next oldest child, Barry, is sixty-four, and my daughters — well, I won't say their ages. To me, they'll always be kids. But I also have a forty-year-old grandson among the brood, all of whom are inching up the actuarial table. They may be asking themselves how they will know when they are old. They may even be looking at me for signs.

I don't want anyone to waste the time, so I'll point out the obvious. I used to be six-foot-two, and now I am five-foot-eleven. Where did those three inches go? Medically, I've been told that vertebrae compact, the skeleton compresses, and you shrink. But I still think of those inches like socks that disappear in the dryer — a mystery. Is that what it means to grow old? You shrink a few inches every few years until you disappear?

Then there's my hair, which used to be brown but is now gray. Actually, it's white. That transformation to Santa Claus–white from dishwater brown wasn't even a speed bump for me. I was touring in *Music Man* at age fifty when I noticed my pate had paled — I was completely white. Instead of being depressed, though, I said to myself, "By God, if I'm ever going to have a chance to look a little like Cary Grant, this is it."

The truth is, my hair could be blue or green for all I care — as long as I have some on my head.

If ever there was a sign I was old, it was when I was rejected by the AARP magazine. That actually happened a few years ago. They asked whether I would be on the cover, and I said, "Sure, why not?" Then I received word that they had changed their mind. They put Michael J. Fox on the cover instead. Apparently, at eighty-six, I was *too old* for AARP. I got over it — immediately — as I do most things.

Losing three inches, not getting a magazine cover — what's the big deal? There are few things in my life I would change, and as a result, I focus on what's next, not the past. Comedian George Burns, who, when asked late in his life whether he lived in the past, said, "No, I live in Beverly Hills. It's much nicer." I live in Malibu and feel the same way. When I do get nostalgic, it's apt to be for simple pleasures, like the jazz and big band standards from the forties and fifties or the kinds of things that make a night special, like a dress code in a nice restaurant or having my Caesar salad dressing made tableside the way I used to enjoy at fine restaurants in the sixties.

If you are suddenly craving a Caesar salad, it might be a sign that you are old. The original Caesar salad dressing that I remember from restaurants was made with raw egg yolks, Worcestershire sauce, and anchovies, and typically mixed and tossed right at the table. I understand that anchovies were added later and weren't part of the original recipe. My wife has learned to make it the way I remember, if anyone wants the recipe. We have it all the time. As a result, I am still enjoying my salad days.

My brother, Jerry, who is six years younger than me, has a slightly different take, partially because he is naturally funny and sees life through a comedic lens. But he has also battled health problems for nearly two decades, from knee replacements (due to his Rafael Nadal–like zeal for chasing down balls on the tennis court) to a liver transplant (while he was on the waiting list, I changed my will to say he could have my liver if I died, and every day he called me to see whether I was still alive). Understandably, those events have taken a toll.

I saw it when he and his wife, Shirley, stayed with us for a couple of months starting last Christmas. While I scooted in and out of the house in my bare feet, as I am known to do (a friend once dubbed me the Barefoot Prince of Malibu), Jerry got around with a cane, the result of a painful back surgery the previous year that had not yet fully healed. It was hard for me to see. I know it was harder for him. One afternoon he landed on the sofa with a heavy sigh.

"How're you doing today?" I asked.

"Terrible," he said.

"What's bothering you?"

"Same thing as yesterday — I'm eighty-three years old!"

"Jer, is there anything good about getting older?" I asked.

"No."

"What about the lessons you've learned?"

"I'm very sorry to say there aren't any."

"Do you have any advice for people who are getting older, who are entering their sixties, seventies, eighties, and nineties?

"Don't do it."

"Don't do what?"

"Don't get older."

What my brother meant was don't slow down, don't give up the things you like to do, don't pay attention to the calendar. In other words, keep moving, stay active, and continue to pursue the interests and activities that keep your spirit young. Jerry is a perfect example. Like me, he blew past sixty-five without thinking of retirement (at the time, he was still playing Luther on the sitcom *Coach*). He's continued to work into his eighties, slowing only when his health refused to cooperate. A couple of years ago he was booked at a club in Palm Springs.

There was just one problem: he hadn't done his stand-up act in a while and couldn't remember his material. A day or two before, he called from his home in Arkansas, asking whether I remembered any of the jokes.

"From twenty-five years ago?" I said.

"Yeah."

"There's nothing written down?"

"No."

He went on anyway. A few days later I ran into Gary Mule Deer, the veteran comedian and musician, who had been at the show. He said my brother had the audience laughing nonstop. According to Gary, there wasn't a person in the theater who didn't have a good time. Though not surprised, I called my brother and asked how he'd managed without his act.

"Shirley," he said, referring to his wife, "remembered my act."

"And you?"

"Not a clue."

"What'd you do?"

"She was just offstage, and I kept yelling to her, 'What do I do now?' Right in the middle of a song too."

Most recently Jerry has had a recurring role on *The Middle,* an ABC comedy about a middle-class Indiana family. He plays actress Patricia Heaton's cantankerous father. Over the Christmas break, while at our house, Jerry pitched the show's executive producers on having me guest star with him on an episode. We shot it a couple of months later, as soon as they finished writing it. We played feuding brothers trying to mend fences before it's too late. But when I show up to visit, my energy and agility piss him off — which is similar to our real-life relationship.

For years he's said that people stop him in airports and restaurants and say, "Hey, Jerry, we loved you on *Coach*. Honey, come here. It's Dick Van Dyke's brother."

Growing up, I didn't make it easy on him. I was a good student (I could have done better, but I was too busy being social), a performer (I starred in most of the school plays: I was taller than the girls and could be heard in the back row), and student body president and then a DJ at the local radio station before going out on the road as one half of a musical-comedy pantomime act. At sixteen, Jerry visited me in Los Angeles, where I was working nightclubs. Impressed, he returned home to Danville and began doing my act. As he says, "I stole the whole thing, went back and made a fortune — at least $25."

He still has a letter I sent him following that visit, saying I couldn't wait to get back to Danville to see his act — "the act you stole from me!" In it I also advised him to get out of nightclubs. "If you stay in night-clubs, you're going to meet a lot of lousy jerks and die broke. The coming thing is television. We should try to get into tele-vision because it should be going great guns."

I was so gung ho about this new device that I took a correspondence course in television repair as a backup in case show business didn't work out for me. I urged Jerry to do the same. But he refused to consider a backup plan. "I was afraid if I had one, I would back into it," he recently explained to me.

And now? Any regrets? "It is what it is," he said with a shrug. "I'm still here." And still waxing philosophic about the lessons he learned along the way, starting with this one: "People worry too much about things that don't matter."

"Like what?" I asked.

"Stuff — the stuff we think other people are going to notice or talk about. As it turns out, nobody gives a crap."

"That's one of the advantages of age," I

said. "You don't worry about what other people think. There's more honesty as the years go by."

Jerry nodded. "That's why I don't understand plastic surgery," he said. "All my friends are getting work done. They come up to me and ask, 'How do I look?' I say, 'I don't know. Who are you?' You can only go so far. People have this idea that they can fix everything. But they only fix what they see, and as you get older, it's the parts you can't see that need to be fixed — like your ass. Never mind your face. Your face is fine. As you get older, it's your ass that disappears. And you don't know that until one day you can't get up and realize you're sitting on your back."

Ladies and gentlemen: my brother.

For me, it is all about how I feel on the inside. These days most of us seventy-, eighty-, and ninety-year-olds feel younger than we are, and the new reality is more like a new honesty: it doesn't matter what we look like on the outside — whether we have gray hair, no hair, less hair, hearing aids, bifocals or trifocals, stooped shoulders, or orthopedic shoes instead of Florsheims or Ferragamos. Our reflections barely matter. After a certain point age doesn't matter. Why even count? For that matter, why even look in the mirror with a critical eye?

You get to that place where you are like a favorite old flannel shirt — well worn, faded, thin in places, but so perfectly comfortable you love it more than anything else in the closet. Like that old shirt, you want to feel great. The outside doesn't matter as much as the texture and touch, all the memories and miles, and, of course, the fact that it still does its job!

At seventy-five, I thought about entering the Senior Olympics. I had been a high jumper in high school, and I felt as good as I did back then. I still ran about a twelve-second hundred-meter and knew I could beat most guys in my age group. If I hadn't taken a job instead, I might have a gold medal on my mantel.

With the right attitude, age is immaterial. At eighty-nine, I became the executive creative producer of the Malibu Playhouse. The opportunity was unexpected, but I thought, "Why not try?" The playhouse is small: a stage, no curtain, just the bare bones of a theater. But ask anyone who works in theater, and they'll tell you there's no limit to the imagination. I have ideas for a sing-along night, a salute to Broadway, and I have spoken to Shirley Jones, Lou Gossett Jr., and others in the neighborhood.

Ed Asner, at age eighty-five, recently finished a show. I know many talented people still eager to work. I am going to sign them up.

Only my brother has been skeptical of this new position, and I know that if his back weren't killing him, he'd be pitching me on the two of us doing *The Sunshine Boys* again. In 2011 we costarred in the Neil Simon classic to raise funds for the theater, and then we took the play on the road for a few nights. We had a blast.

I remember walking into a scene one night, hunched over, and my brother whispered, "Dick, you don't have to *play* old anymore."

It broke me up. It also began a conversation between the two of us that we recently continued:

"Jer, at what age did you begin to think of yourself as old?"

"This age."

"Really?"

"It was just like, 'Oh, shit, I can't be eighty-three. I can't be.' "

"What happened that made you feel that way? Your knees? Your back?"

"No, it was that my phone stopped ringing. I used to be on the phone constantly. I had a lot of friends. Then all of a sudden . . ."

"Do you remember our mother saying the same thing? She complained that everyone was gone. She had no one with whom she could talk about the past. I know what she meant. I had to have all my suits taken in because I'm shrinking. I have the same tailor as George Hamilton. I ran into him at a banquet dinner and asked, 'How's our tailor?' He said, 'He's dead.' "

"It's been like that since I came out here. Everybody I have asked about, I find out they're dead." Jerry paused. "On the bright side, they are, and I'm not."

The two of us fell silent and sipped our coffee. I thought about my good fortune at still being able to sing, dance, travel, and do nearly everything else I have enjoyed my entire life. I adore my wife, four kids, seven grandchildren, and great-grandchildren. Jerry, too, despite his recent physical problems, has had a long, happy marriage and a full life. Pretty good for two guys with a combined age of 172 years.

"Jer, I have one more question," I said.

"Shoot."

"How do you know when you're old?"

"If I shut my eyes, I still feel twenty-five," he said. "Does that tell you something?"

It did. Then I told him about a dream I

have frequently, usually just before I wake up. In the dream I am running through an open field, running like a deer — free and fast and wide open without ever getting tired. I dream that a lot, probably because I can't run like that anymore. It is a spectacular dream: therapeutic, thrilling, energizing, and fun. Then I wake up feeling —"

"Like a kid," Jerry said.

"Yes, exactly like I did as a kid."

"And are you disappointed when you get up and look in the mirror?"

I shook my head. It is wonderful to remember the feeling of being young, but if you ask me, it's much more important to revel in what you still have.

THAT OLD SENILITY

These are lyrics I rewrote to the classic Disney song "The Bare Necessities" by Terry Gilkyson from the 1967 movie *The Jungle Book.* I hope you enjoy singing them as much as I do.

I've got that old senility,
that simple old senility.
Forgot about my trouble and my strife.

I mean that old senility.
I lost my old ability
to recognize my neighbors or my wife.

Wherever I wander,
wherever I roam
I go too far yonder
and can't find my way home.

My glasses may be on my head.
I look everywhere else instead.
And then I look behind the door
and find the pair that I lost before.

That old senility
will come to you.

Mr. Vandy Dances Again

"I almost died." This is something you hear older people say on occasion — the lucky ones, obviously. Count me as one of the lucky ones.

I didn't know I almost died until afterward, of course, when my wife told me. Someone else always has to tell you. If they didn't say something, if they didn't fill you in on the horrific details ("Oh, there were tubes, and beeping machines, you didn't move, and the doctors couldn't answer any of my questions — it wasn't good"), there would be no way of knowing how close you came to following the proverbial white light to that special place where there are no middle seats, no flat tires, and no extra-long hairs growing out of your ears.

Having said that, I can't vouch for the details of the afterlife. I made up the part about no middle seats, no long hairs growing out of your ears, and so on. Everyone has their own version of an afterlife without mortal inconveniences. According to what I have read, though, we do seem to sail into an all-encompassing bright light when we leave this life, and it is reported to be a comforting experience, like a loving hug from your mother after you've been gone the whole day. But none of that happened to me when I was down. My body was present, but I was gone. When I try to think of what that was like, I hit a blank spot. The words that come to mind are gray, cardboard, empty, and dull. Not bright. Not white. Not light.

It was February 2014, and my wife, Arlene, and I were in Vancouver, where I was working on *Night at the Museum: Secret of the Tomb,* the third installment in this fun, family-oriented series of adventure movies. I was in perfect health when I got up there. Like every actor, I took a physical before the job for insurance purposes. I passed with flying colors.

"I wish I felt as good," the doctor said as he shook my hand.

On the set I worked with Ben Stiller and Mickey Rooney. We were scheduled for a two-day shoot on location in an assisted-living facility, a place that would have, in a less politically correct time, been called an old folks' home. I was supposed to dance a salsa with three ladies from a local dance school. None of them were professional dancers, and to be candid, I am a fake. People think I am a trained dancer — I'm not. I am best when I freestyle, when I can go with the way the music makes me feel.

How do I explain *Bye Bye Birdie* and *Mary Poppins*? Easy: I was fortunate to work with Gower Champion and Mark and Dee Dee Wood, brilliant choreographers who crafted dance numbers around what I *could* do. This is one of the reasons I say no to *Dancing with the Stars* every time they call — and they have called several times. The physical undertaking aside, I would have to learn a new dance every week, and I would have trouble doing that at the level I would expect of myself.

For the "Step in Time" number in *Mary Poppins,* we rehearsed for six weeks. On *Night at the Museum,* I only had one day to learn to salsa. It wasn't enough for the dance to sink in and become second nature. I should also mention that I can't lead. Well, I can — but I shouldn't. On the set we did numerous takes, and I could tell the dance wasn't coming off the way everyone hoped.

Out of the corner of my eye I saw Shawn Levy, the director, quietly pulling at his hair, frustrated, while over in the wings, Ben Stiller waited, and waited, and waited for his cue to walk into the scene. But we never got to that point.

Finally Arlene stepped onto the set and said what we all were thinking: "This isn't working." She suggested I give up the salsa and freestyle instead. The director agreed, though I needed more persuasion before I released the awkward hold on my dance partner. I didn't want to disappoint my dance partners or the people who had worked on the dance itself.

"What about the choreography?" I asked.

Arlene shook her head. "I don't think they care as much about the specific steps as they do about seeing you dance in your style."

I looked around. The director, the choreographer, and my fellow actors were nodding in agreement. Arlene suggested that the soundman cue up the hit "Blurred Lines," and as soon as the opening bars played over the loud speakers, the director looked at me and said, "Just let yourself go."

I did — and the rest happened in a single take.

Ben Stiller was impressed. "What the hell do you do?" he said. "Is it vitamins? Did you make a pact with the Devil? What is it? I can't get over that you're eighty-eight years old and still jumping around!"

I did not plan to slow down either. After that scene wrapped, Arlene and I were looking forward to another week in Vancouver. Then I was scheduled to begin work on the new Hallmark TV series *Signed, Sealed, Delivered.* But two days later I was fighting for my life. That's how quickly and unexpectedly things can change. It's also a reminder of why today is always more important than tomorrow.

Here's what happened: Arlene and I spent the morning touring the city and stopped for lunch at the Old Spaghetti Factory in Vancouver's historic Gastown District. On the walk back to the hotel I grew weak and winded. I thought it might be because we were going up a slight hill. Then the slight hill felt like a mountain. Several times I stopped to catch my breath. I thought, "My God, I'm not going to make it."

By nighttime I was quite ill. I was running a fever and did not have the energy to get out of bed. How could this be, when two days earlier I had danced for hours on the movie set? Arlene summoned a local doctor, who gave me medicine to reduce my temperature. The second I took it, though, I was knocked out. From what Arlene later told me, I was down the rest of that night and the entire next day.

Two days later I opened my eyes again and saw my wife sitting at my bedside, coaxing me back to the world of the living. I am convinced that I would have died if Arlene hadn't been taking care of me that whole time.

The following day I was able to sit up in bed and get to the bathroom on my own. Those little things were suddenly significant achievements. Later that week I was supposed to begin work on *Signed, Sealed, Delivered,* but Arlene informed the production company that I was ill. They sent a doctor to the hotel. After a few more days in bed, I relapsed, not dramatically, but to the point that Arlene took me to the ER, where I was diagnosed with pneumonia.

Even though every breath was a painful struggle, I had a hard time accepting the reality of the diagnosis. The previous month I had come down with shingles, which turned into weeks of torturous pain and itching. But I soldiered through it. Now the deal was pneumonia: this was serious. How did I get pneumonia? I was not used to being sick. I didn't know how to be sick. It was not in my repertoire. The word "sick" wasn't even in my vocabulary. The closest I came to being sick was back in my early sixties when I had gone for a physical. A routine chest X-ray showed what the doctor described as "emphysema scars."

"I have emphysema?" I asked, frightened.

"The beginning stages," he said.

I immediately thought of my father, a heavy smoker, who had died of emphysema. At the time I was also a two- or three-pack-a-day smoker — until that moment. I quit then and there, and for the next thirty-plus years I went full bore without missing a step, until Vancouver — and then wham!

On the flight back to Los Angeles I tried to understand where and how I could have gotten pneumonia. It could've been at the assisted-living facility, where I took time to meet and greet the residents, shaking hands, signing autographs, and posing for pictures. I might have also picked up a bug in a restaurant, a taxi, or at the hotel. It was impossible to say, and you can't live your life in fear of getting sick. I decided it was fate — payback for eighty-eight straight years of feeling terrific.

At home my recovery was slow. I didn't bounce back after a few days, as I was used to doing with a cold or the flu. I supposed this was the downside of getting sick later in life. Then I had a setback. One day while Arlene was out doing errands, I felt my heart rate speed up, and my breathing became labored. I thought, "Heart attack." I called my doctor, who had me drive in and sent me straight to X-ray. As he had suspected on the phone, I had a collapsed lung.

I phoned Arlene and gave her an update. She asked whether I wanted her — or needed her — to come get me. "No, they're going to do a little procedure," I said. "Then I'll be able to drive home." I had one request: Could she pick up my new prescription at the pharmacy? Otherwise, I said I'd see her soon.

As it turned out, we saw each other an hour and a half later in the pharmacy parking lot, where I stopped unexpectedly because the pain medication from the procedure had started to wear off while I was driving home, and I wanted my pills as soon as possible. Arlene saw me get out of the car clutching my side. Knowing I was in pain and realizing I had underplayed my condition, she hurried over to me to see what was really wrong.

"Don't worry. I'm fine," I said.

"What's that . . . that —" She pointed at the plastic tube hanging out of my side, another detail I hadn't mentioned to her.

"It's a valve — to help re-inflate the lung,"

I said. "It's temporary."

Over the next couple months my lung collapsed two more times. The second time my doctor did a pleurodesis, a more extensive procedure in which he glued my lung to my chest wall. The third time it turned out I needed some additional gluing due to having extra long lungs — they'd missed a portion. But that did the trick, and I spent the rest of the winter and all spring recuperating. It took months for me to regain the weight and strength I lost during the ordeal. I benefitted from the patience and support of a loving wife and family who encouraged me to get back to the things I loved to do, which I think is the key to recovery. Get back to what you love to do.

What I realized is that age is directly related to health. If you feel physically fit, age is immaterial, as it had always been for me. I had gone from dancing like I was in my forties to feeling nearly dead to trudging around the house like I was one hundred–plus, until gradually I was back to feeling not just younger but normal. Back to where I no longer thought about my age. My brother marveled at my resiliency.

"I don't know how anyone pulls through when they have to lie on those beds in the hospital," he said.

"Oh my God, they're uncomfortable," I concurred.

"Many people fall out of those beds and break their butt," he said. "Thank God that didn't happen to you."

In May I started going to the gym again, forcing myself at first, but knowing it was vital to get back to my routine of lifting weights and walking on the treadmill if I wanted to get my stamina back — which I did.

Arlene noted the difference one day after lunch. I was at the kitchen sink, doing dishes, and we were singing "Carolina in the Morning." She said, "Wow, did you hear that?" I looked at her curiously, not having heard anything other than our harmonizing. "You held that note a long time — longer than me! I think that's a sign your lungs are back to normal."

With age comes a constantly changing sense of normal. But each one of us determines our own sense of normal, and mine was defined by the sheer delight I felt at having survived. One afternoon Arlene and I were at a store picking up running shoes, and I started to dance. I heard music playing, and my body began to move. It was involuntary, as if my body was saying, "Hey, I'm back! And I still know all the moves."

Arlene captured it on her phone and posted the video on Twitter.

"The wait is over," she wrote. "Mr. Vandy Dances." The video went viral instantly. "This made my day!" one fan commented. *People* magazine called it mesmerizing. And actor Denis Leary retweeted the video with the caption, "Father Time can suck it."

I felt the same way — and still do.

Dancing with Your Inner Child — A Workout for Older People

I am a child in search of his inner adult, though the truth is that I'm not searching too hard. I don't recommend anyone doing so. That is the secret, the one people always ask me about when they see me singing and dancing, whistling my way through the grocery store or doing a soft shoe in the checkout line. They say, "Pardon me, Mr. Van Dyke, but you seem so happy. What's your secret?"

What they really want to know is how I have managed to grow old, even very old, without growing up, and the answer is this: I haven't grown up. I play. I dance with my inner child. Every day.

There.

Now you know the secret too.

If you don't sing and dance like me, figure out how your inner child likes to play and then make a date to do so.

I was onto this idea years ago. When we

were shooting *The Dick Van Dyke Show,* I played Rob Petrie, a man with adult mannerisms and responsibilities — he was a husband, father, and breadwinner — who also had the insecurity and willfulness of a child. He approached work and life with childlike openness and enthusiasm, wary of authority, worried that something could go wrong but always ready to have fun. In many ways he was like me, I suppose.

He was also like the man who created him on paper, my good friend Carl Reiner, who is another man who has grown old without losing the brilliant curiosity of his youth. Scripture says you should put aside childish things when you grow up. I take that to mean willfulness, self-centeredness, and things like that — not imagination, creativity, and joyful curiosity.

I am not alone here. I read online that billionaire octogenarian Warren Buffet reportedly eats like a six-year-old. He guzzles Cokes and says his diet is also high in salt. I am going to guess he eats hamburgers and fries too. When you are eighty-five like Mr. Buffet — or my age, soon to be ninety — I say eat whatever you want, whenever you want . . . in moderation, of course. Or not in moderation if it is a special occasion, like lunch or dinner or a snack in between meals.

According to one story, Mr. Buffet researched actuarial tables and found that six-year-olds have the lowest death rate, so he decided to eat like a kid. Whether that is 100 percent true is beside the point to me because the message it conveys is spot-on: keep your inner child alive and well. Dance with it. Take it out to lunch. Indulge it. Do whatever it takes. Mr. Buffet famously treats himself to Dairy Queen. I like a nightly ice cream sundae, too, of Häagen Dazs® vanilla ice cream topped with Hershey's chocolate syrup. Hey, we may be onto something here!

My inner child is all about playtime, and I know why. Some of my fondest memories are of the summers I spent when school got out. I can't believe how many years have passed since then, but the smells and feel of those June days are still so fresh that they might as well have happened the day before yesterday. I would count down the last days of the school year, and as soon as vacation started, I'd kick off my shoes and spend the next two and a half months running through fields, playing, and doing whatever I felt like doing.

This was before e-mail and social media, before electronic games, before cell phones, even before television! The days seemed to have more time, and I used that time much as I do now — to imagine and create, to play. I wanted to be a magician. I ordered tricks in the mail for 25 cents from the Johnson & Smith catalog and practiced my sleight-of-hand for hours in the basement. All that practice paid off when I was hired for $3 to perform at the Kiwanis Club.

At age ten I got my first bicycle, a rusty two-wheeler I found in a pawn shop downtown for $7. Even at that price, my dad said he couldn't afford it on his traveling salesman's salary, this still being the tail-end of the Great Depression. But after much pleading on my part, he bought it for me. That bike meant everything to me. I cleaned it off, rubbed off the rust, oiled it up, rode it to my friend's house, and then, eventually, out to the lake, which was several miles way. Suddenly I had freedom — and that changed my life.

These days my playtime is more structured than it was when I was a kid, and it's slower paced — there's no running through open fields or riding my bike to the lake. But my days still include singing, dancing, drawing, and playing games. Children are taught to amuse themselves. They're told to "go play." I'm all in favor of refresher courses for adults. As seniors, it is vital to have hobbies and passions, to have playtime, and to engage in them every day.

I wouldn't tell anyone to do exactly as I do, but maybe my daily schedule can provide some ideas. Consider:

1. In the morning I work out at my local gym. I'll be honest, every day it gets tougher to get out of bed, put on the sweats, and work out. But it's important. And that first cup of coffee I have plays a crucial part in getting me out the door. I've been going to my gym for so long that they gave me a set of keys so I can open up if I arrive early. To warm up, I hang upside down and stretch. Then I spend time on the treadmill before lifting weights. Some days I alternate: lift, then aerobics.

Not too long ago, when I was on the treadmill, the guy next to me said, "Hey, you're humming! The rest of us are huffing and puffing and you're humming. How do you do that?"

Half-jokingly, I said, "Vocal chords are muscles too." But also humming, as with a Buddhist chanting, singing, or even an infant making noises as it discovers its voice, sets up a sympathetic frequency in your body that simply feels good.

Try it: mmmmmmmmm.

Anyway. I am never going to look like Mr.

Universe, but I seem to be getting stronger, especially since recovering from pneumonia. I am lifting more weight than I have in a few years. The younger guys at the gym are impressed that I can lift my age and sometimes even more, though, as I tell them, we'll see if that is still true in ten or twenty years. I just know I like to feel good, to feel in shape, and I always have.

Back in my Air Force days I got one of the highest fitness ratings in the state of Texas. I couldn't run distances, but I was always the first one through the obstacle course. But that was natural, youthful ability. I started working out more on a more regular basis when I was doing *Bye Bye Birdie* on Broadway in 1960. One afternoon, a matinee day, I saw all the dancers working out with weights. I started joining them between shows. I was thirty-four or thirty-five years old. I felt so good that I kept it up and haven't stopped.

Good habits matter. Eating light and fresh. Staying away from fast and processed foods. Not smoking. Working out regularly. Even going for a walk every day is extremely beneficial for longevity, according to studies I have heard on the news. As pianist Eubie Blake said when he was performing at age ninety-nine, "If I'd known I was going to live this long, I'd have taken better care of myself." Times have changed. Plan on living long, and start when you're young so that by the time you're my age, the right diet and exercise and other good habits are second nature.

2. After the gym I go to the grocery store to pick up assorted items my wife and I need that day. As I push my cart up and down the aisles, I often sing and dance to the music playing in the background. Most of the time I'm not aware I'm doing this, but apparently the people working there look forward to my visits as entertainment. If for some reason I don't sing or dance, I hear from the store manager or Debbie, my favorite checker. "Hey, Dick, why aren't you singing? Why aren't you dancing?" That is the question I pose to other people, including you, the reader, literally and metaphorically: If you aren't singing or dancing, why not?

3. Back home I check my To-Do list for the rest of the day. I make it out the night before and then add to it as the day goes on. I always have a list of tasks. Though I never get through all of them, the worst is when I get to the market and can't read my own writing. But it's like a job. I am a maintenance man for my own life. Actually, as I think about it, that's a job one should assume and take more seriously with age. Take care of things at home. As Shakespeare wrote, "Our remedies often in ourselves do lie, which we ascribe to heaven: the fated sky." So every day I make To-Do lists.

1. Put gas in the car!!
2. Call Bill — need some backing tracks.
3. Make a haircut appointment!!
4. Get gum.
5. Find Blu-ray burner for 3D animations.
6. Get blue blazer tailored.
7. Movie tonight? Ask Arlene.

I also suggest making a high-level, more philosophical To Do list.

1. Never go down the stairs sideways.
2. Try to understand why time keeps speeding up.
3. Wake up your sixth sense.
4. Keep learning.
5. Find your song — and sing it!!!
6. What's new?

And then there is the list nobody makes,

the NOT To-Do list.

1. Do not forget to exercise.
2. Do not stop being curious.
3. Do not forget to try new things — even a new flavor of ice cream will do.
4. Do not forget to open your mind every day.
5. Do not stop asking why do I believe what I believe.
6. Do not forget to smile.
7. Do not forget to make someone else smile.

4. Then I do the crossword puzzle to exercise my brain. Studies have shown that the brain is a use-it-or-lose-it organ. To keep it flexible and in good working order, it must be used, stimulated, even challenged. I have always believed that crossword puzzles are one of the best ways to exercise your brain. However, although they are indeed effective, they aren't number one. I read a study in the *New England Journal of Medicine* on the best mental and physical activities for staying sharp in old age and preventing dementia, and doing crossword puzzles at least four days a week was the second-best thing you can do stay clear and present.

Guess which one of the following was the best thing you can do to stay sharp as you age.

a. Playing cards
b. Solving math problems
c. Dancing
d. Baking chocolate chip cookies

The answer is C, dancing — and I promise that I am not making this up. More than any physical or mental activity, moving your feet to a good beat provides the brain with the most fuel to fight the aging process. So guess what I make sure is also on my To-Do list every day?

5. I sing and dance. If I feel like dancing around the house, I use Pandora (my wife introduced me to this fantastic app) to find music with a beat that suits my mood. If I feel like singing, I will sit down at the piano or put on the stereo and sing along. Take a moment to put down this book and try it.
Suggested songs to sing right now:

1. "Jolly Holiday"
2. "Carolina in the Morning"
3. "Simple Melody" (Bing Crosby and Gary Crosby did it, and it's such

73

fun to sing. Arlene and I have started singing it around the house. Look it up if you don't know it.)

4. "On a Wonderful Day Like Today"
5. "I Wish I Was in Love Again"

Suggested songs to dance to right now:

1. "Jolly Holiday"
2. "Tea for Two"
3. "Cheek to Cheek" (I'm picturing Fred Astaire and Ginger Rogers in *Top Hat* as I write this.)
4. "What Is This Thing Called Love?"
5. "Take the A Train"

6. Stay involved in the world — and with other people. It's important to keep up with current events. I watch the news every night — both sides — in case one of them is right. I argue with the right and the left and sometimes the middle too. But staying involved in the world also — and more importantly — means connecting with other people. Loneliness and isolation are major problems for people over sixty-five and typically lead to declining health, depression, and other serious issues. I am not an expert, but I do know the easiest and most meaningful way to counter this is to volunteer.

Whatever you give, you get back many times over, including a sense of purpose, a profound sense that your presence in this world matters. For the past twenty years I have been involved with the Midnight Mission, a Los Angeles–based facility dedicated to helping men, women, and children who have lost everything return to self-sufficiency. I spend every holiday there; I don't get the Christmas spirit until I am at the Mission. Early on I approached a large, mean-looking man and wished him a merry Christmas. The menacing look on his face disappeared — he smiled. "People look through us," he says. "Or they look past us. Nobody sees us. But you're looking right at me. That is one helluva gift, man." His smile was an even bigger gift to me. And it has been that way ever since.

One day Arlene asked whether I had ever taken one of the families to Disneyland. I hadn't, so we arranged with the Mission to host a family at Disneyland for a day. They selected a woman with three children. She had a harrowing background that included drugs, abuse, homelessness, and losing her kids. Through the Mission she turned her life around, landed a job at a department store, where she has been promoted twice, the latest to a manager, and she got her kids, now ages six, five, and three, back and is doing a great job raising them. We all met at California Adventure. I was supposed to go on one ride with them and have lunch. I ended up staying with them for five hours. The children had no idea who I was or my connection to Disney. They had never seen *Mary Poppins.* It didn't matter. We laughed and ate our way through the park. In Tomorrowland I heard the song "Supercalifragilisticexpialidocious" and led them in a sing-along. At the end of our day together the six-year-old girl said, "I had the most fun ever. This is the best day of my life." Of course, the only thing bigger than her smile was mine.

7. I learn something new every day, like lines from Shakespeare. I make time nearly every day to memorize the lines. I started with *King Lear* and enjoyed the sound of my recitations as much as I did the accomplishment of having committed them to memory. The language is beautiful, and the writing is full of truth. "Love is not love when it is mingled with regards that stand aloof from the entire point." One afternoon I went to Carl Reiner's house and surprised my longtime friend by working a few of the Bard's more famous lines into the conversa-

tion. "My gosh, I've known you for fifty years," Carl said. "I had no idea you did Shakespeare." Carl knows Shakespeare as well as any professor. He used to do Shakespearean doubletalk as a comedic bit; in fact, that bit got him transferred from the Army to Special Services in World War II. I have often thought he might be old Bill himself reincarnated in a funnier version — from British to Yiddish, as one of our old *Dick Van Dyke Show* writers once quipped. "To be or not to be" may be the question, but learning should be a lifelong quest. If Shakespeare doesn't ignite your curiosity, find another subject — biology, science, history, literature, comedy, music, cooking — the options are infinite. And good for you. Researchers and doctors speak highly of the value of memorization as an excellent way to keep the mind in tip-top shake. You can do a lot worse than Shakespeare.

8. I take a nap every afternoon just like a child, and I highly recommend this refreshing break in the day to you and everyone else. Most of South America and Europe do the same thing. Try it.

9. I play games. Ralph Waldo Emerson said, "It is a happy talent to know how to play," and I concur. If not for this passion, I might have starved. In 1960, after networks passed on a TV pilot I did and before I was cast in *Bye Bye Birdie* — in other words, at a moment in time when I was without work — my agent got me a job on a game show, Mike Stokey's *Pantomime Quiz.* I was partnered with Carol Burnett and Howard Morris. I knew Carol from *The Garry Moore Show,* and the two of us turned out to be great teammates. We clicked on- and off-screen. Both of us were good at pantomime, and both of us desperately needed the $200 you got for winning the game; it's how we fed our families. We also had a good time. These days I like charades, brain teasers, and anagrams. I have a knack for spotting signs when I drive around town and reordering the letters to make new words. It's like my brain is wired to play, even when I am doing something else. At night Arlene and I watch *Jeopardy* in bed while we eat dinner. She has, on at least half a dozen occasions, blurted out the answer to the Final Jeopardy question before host Alex Trebek has even asked it. I can still hear her saying, "Lord Byron" and then looking at her when that turned out to be right. "I don't even know who Lord Byron is," she said. It's uncanny. As for me, I play the traditional way. I wait to hear the clue. How do I fare? As my old costar Morey Amsterdam once said, "I know a lot. I just can't think of it."

10. At the end of the day I have dessert. I always have dessert. I don't skip it, and neither should you. That's a motto to live by. It might be one for the headstone: "He enjoyed his dessert." As I said earlier, my end-of-the-day treat is vanilla ice cream topped with Hershey's chocolate syrup. After dinner I get out the ice cream and chocolate syrup. The two are the perfect combination: two generous scoops of ice cream, then a healthy pour of Hershey's syrup over the two scoops. They are proof that opposites attract. Interestingly, there are no directions on the can for the right amount. I recommend a slow pour, letting the sauce fall onto the top of each scoop and slowly cascade down the sides. Keep pouring until there is a generous pool of syrup at the bottom of the dish, just enough so that it appears the ice cream is resting on a thin sheet of chocolate. Then wait two minutes before eating. This does two things. First, it allows the ice cream to melt into the sauce, which enhances the flavor. Second, it increases the anticipation of the first bite. Pay no attention to the nutritional information on the ice cream or the chocolate sauce. Dessert is about rewarding yourself with something sweet: a just dessert at the end of the day. As Thornton Wilder, the great playwright, put it, "My advice to you is not to inquire why or whither, but just enjoy your ice cream while it's on your plate."

Enjoy the Ride
(FOR MY FRIEND BOB PALMER)

We took a cruise to Alaska, and it didn't turn out the way we expected. Arlene and I had hoped for something special. We got something else instead. We got a mix — wonders and warts. But you know what? That is okay. That's life. As people get older, part of the challenge is to maintain the enthusiasm of our younger days for new experiences, for living life. Travel pushes you out of your comfort zone. It is fraught with experiences that don't work out as planned, testing your mettle and resiliency and reminding you that life constantly throws us curves, not the least of which, after a certain age, are eyes that can't read menus in the dark, knees that refuse to bend when we want them to, and patience that disappears when we most need it.

In our case the curves had to do with toilets that didn't work and a cruise that didn't live up to the photos in the brochure.

Basically, our two weeks away from home weren't perfect. But, as I said, what is?

Our trip in September 2014 was supposed to be a make-up-for-lost-time-slash-thank-you to my wife for her patience, care, and affection during the past seven months while I battled back from pneumonia and shingles. We'd booked a cruise to Alaska earlier in the year; my illness had forced us to cancel. Now, back at full strength, I wanted to have some fun. I wanted to take Arlene to Alaska and show her the awe-inspiring wilderness and wildlife. I'd gone there on a cruise years before, but she'd never been. You don't realize the scale or the beauty of that frozen frontier until you're staring at it in person; then it can be life changing. Arlene was going to love it.

I booked us on the last cruise of the season. In a way the timing seemed more apropos than before because now the trip overlapped with Arlene's forty-third birthday. A few weeks before we departed, our tickets arrived in fancy silver boxes with our names engraved on the lid, along with a brochure showing couples in white terry cloth robes on a veranda with a butler offering drinks and food. We very easily pictured ourselves on that veranda. We were excited.

As it turned out, we probably should have

stopped there, with the fantasy created by the brochures. Reality rarely lives up to those kinds of pictures. In addition, right before we left we got word that my closest friend and longtime publicist, Bob Palmer, was going into the hospital for minor heart surgery to adjust his pacemaker. I wished him well, and Arlene e-mailed his daughter, saying we'd check in with her for an update. Looking back, that might've been an omen, but we were full-speed ahead — and eager to get going.

At my son Chris's suggestion, we traveled from Los Angeles to Vancouver, the starting point of our cruise, via train. He said the thirty-six-hour rail journey up the coast afforded breathtaking views and was worth the extra time. We were sold. Time is the only real luxury all of us have, and because we weren't in a hurry, why not enjoy it? We boarded the Superliner, as the train was called, in LA's historic Union Station, the location of many old movies and, oddly, a site I had never visited. We found our private room on the second floor and headed to the sightseeing lounge.

By early afternoon we were enjoying views of the coastline near Santa Barbara. Everything was as we imagined. Then Arlene went to our room to use the bathroom and came back a short time later shaking her head.

"It's broken," she said.

"What is?" I asked.

"The toilet."

"That isn't good. Did you speak to someone about it?"

"The attendant wasn't much help. He said they might be able to get it fixed when we're in Oakland."

I looked at my watch. Arlene was already ahead of me.

"Yeah, that's five or six hours from now."

Our conductor looked like he was straight out of *The Polar Express* — portly, bespectacled, white hair, friendly — and he tried to accommodate us by offering us use of the room next to ours. In fact, he pulled open the adjoining wall and turned our berth into a plush, two-bedroom suite. The only trouble was the toilet in that other room didn't work either. It turned out the toilets in the entire car were out of order. Needless to say, the first leg of the trip, to Seattle, was a long one.

But we got there, and the next day we got to Vancouver and found our ship, which was larger than I had imagined, considering there were only 350 passengers total. The ship looked as if it were meant to accommodate ten times that number. Our quarters were nice, the toilet worked, but the emergency procedures drill we practiced that first afternoon, as is routine on ships, raised a small red flag when I noticed the majority of passengers didn't look very lively, even though I was probably the oldest passenger onboard.

"Uh oh," I whispered to Arlene.

"It will get better," she said.

I had my concerns. For the next two days we were at sea. No stops. Surrounded by water. With nothing of interest to us happening on the ship. And that's the risk of a cruise. You're trapped. My brother performed on cruise ships for years before he was on *Coach.* They provided a good living. He only had to work a few nights, and the rest of the time on the ship was his to spend as he wished. But it was hit or miss, depending on the audience. He once played the last week of a world cruise. He met the ship for the final week of what had been a three- or four-month adventure.

He did his act, and he bombed. But bombing on a ship, he explained, was worse than anyplace else. "If you lay an egg in a nightclub, you get to go home," he said. "On a cruise you have to live with the audience for the rest of the week. Everywhere I went, I saw their disappointment. There was no escape."

And that's the way we felt for those two days. There was no music anywhere on board, no Internet or cable TV. It was eerily quiet, even during the day. Arlene and I both agreed that it was like being on the set of *The Shining* at sea. Activities included golf lessons — but we don't play golf — and seminars on health ("What do your feet say about your health?") and shopping ("How to buy diamonds"). They didn't interest us either. There was also a casino, but we don't gamble. Neither did most of the passengers — whenever we would walk by, there were two or maybe three people playing the slot machines. No one playing cards, craps, roulette, or whatever you play at those big green tables (I told you I don't gamble).

On the plus side, the food was delicious, and that was a distraction we welcomed after Arlene suffered a panic attack upon seeing nothing but water in every direction. It happened toward the end of that first day and then got worse at night when we hit some rough water. Arlene's previous boating experience consisted of the Circle Line Ferry in New York, the Catalina Express, and the party boat we rented for her fortieth birthday. It took her a bit to get used to being at sea.

"My mind is fixated on all the things that could happen," she explained. "Hypothermia. Sharks. Drowning."

I did whatever I could to calm her fears and relieve her from visions of what she called "a watery grave." I told her about my first cruise in the 1960s. I was filming a movie in Europe, and my then-wife, Margie, our daughter Stacy, and I crossed the Atlantic on a German ship called the *Bremen*. I thought it would be fun and relaxing, but the crew was stiff and unfriendly. Everything was "Achtung!"

The sommelier seemed angry the war had ended. One night, in an effort to make conversation, I asked him a question about the ship, something along the lines of, "This is the second *Bremen,* isn't it? Wasn't there another *Bremen*?"

"Yes, there was," he said.

"I thought so," I nodded. "What happened to it?"

"You sunk it," he snapped.

After a good night's sleep, Arlene's anxiety passed, and the adventure picked up when we got to Alaska. In Juneau we transferred to a small boat for an amazing day of whale watching. We watched with awe as a group of beautiful giants breached the water and slapped the surface with their enormous tales. Seeing a sight like that quickly adds perspective to your place in the world.

The galley on the tiny boat also served some of the best hamburgers I had ever tasted. We spent the next day docked in Skagway and took a charming trolley car tour around town. Later, while I returned to the boat, Arlene stayed in town to get some souvenirs and decided to take a tour of the Red Onion Saloon, a former bordello that wasn't, as she told me, "listed in our fancy-pants tour guide."

As she waited for her tour guide, an old man wandered inside. She told me that he looked like Rip Van Winkle — with long gray hair, a beard, and a walking cane — or perhaps he *was* Rip Van Winkle, and the Red Onion was still functioning as a brothel when he went to sleep. He stepped toward Arlene and got her attention.

"How much is it?" he asked.

"Ten dollars," she said, thinking he was asking about the tour.

"Ten dollars?!" Arlene realized he was trying to get a girl and must have thought that ten bucks was too much — if he could've gotten a girl, which he couldn't.

Arlene set him straight. "It's not a functioning brothel," she said.

"Do you know where I could get a girl?"

he then asked.

"No, I don't know."

Arlene assumed he saw her wedding ring, but maybe not, as he asked, "Are you married?"

"VERY," she said — and that's when the tour guide appeared and Rip Van Winkle sauntered out of the building. While walking around Skagway, Arlene enjoyed listening to what she thought were local street musicians but with further investigation discovered they were jazz musicians from the Jazz Cruise that was practically on the same exact route as our Snooze Cruise! Boy, were we tempted to jump ship!

Other highlights included the Mendenhall Glacier, more whale watching in Sitka, the wilderness in Prince Rupert, British Columbia, and a private tour of the Parliament Building in Victoria, which was not planned. Arlene and I were parked in front of the building, marveling at the neo-Baroque and Renaissance architecture of the historic landmark, when a cop asked us to move the car. Then he recognized me, and soon we were being escorted to a VIP line inside.

In the end two things about the trip stand out to me. First, every day we were on the ocean we saw a school of dolphins swimming next to our boat. Anytime something seemed to bother us, we would look out at those beautiful, graceful creatures and somehow instantly feel better. The other thing is the laughs Arlene and I shared. We laughed all the time, especially when things went wrong. That ability to laugh made the trip.

It was only when we got off the boat for good in Vancouver that we encountered a real problem. Arlene went online and found an e-mail from Bob Palmer's daughter. It turned out that my friend was not doing well following what was supposed to be routine surgery. "He's at peace with what's happening," his daughter wrote.

Concerned about being able to say good-bye, we caught the first available flight back to Los Angeles and went straight to Bob's house. We sat at his bedside and had a nice two-hour visit. The next day he lapsed into a coma and never woke up.

I already missed him, and the long, almost daily conversations we would have about everything from old movies and songs to the meaning of life. He was a supremely intelligent man who had worked in TV and movies for stars such as Anthony Hopkins and Faye Dunaway and also for studios. He had served in the Navy. He was a writer. He was a great friend. And later I was reminded that he had been born in Alaska.

I so wished I could have told him about our trip. He knew how much I had been looking forward to taking Arlene to see that breathtaking scenery. We had spoken about both of our previous cruises and vacations. Like me, he was in his eighties, and between the two of us, we had taken many excursions — some wonderful, some we would not repeat, but none we would forget. To me, that's the point — and both of us said as much to each other. The food isn't always perfect, sometimes you get lost, sometimes it rains . . . but it's all okay. As Arlene and I also concluded, that's life.

Despite the bumps and wrong turns, enjoy the ride.

Rewriting the Rules

It was a sunny afternoon, and I was strolling along Robertson Drive in Beverly Hills. The meetings that had brought me into town were finished, and I thought a walk past all the fancy stores would be fun — and it was. The sidewalks were crowded with fashionably dressed people, a few of whom said hello, causing me to smile and say hello back, which made the world seem smaller and friendlier than it normally comes across on, say, the local news.

As I passed the Tommy Hilfiger store something in the window caught my eye. I went inside for a closer look but quickly got the impression that the store wasn't used to customers my age. Otherwise, I can't imagine why the young saleswoman, after seeing me looking around, would have approached me and said, "Sir, I don't think you'll find anything here that you'll like."

It was not my first encounter with ageism,

but it was the most blatant. Typically the remarks are subtler. Someone will come up to me and say, "Wow, you look good." What they really mean is that they are surprised I am alive. Nobody said I "looked good" when I was thirty-five. Or someone will ask whether I have trouble remembering my lines or need cue cards written in EXTRA-LARGE TYPE or require a wheelchair getting to the elevator. Then there are the jokes we've all heard: "What were Adam and Eve like?" "Do you need help blowing out your birthday candles?" "At your age, I bet your back goes out more than you do."

I get it. I've heard them — and more. And most of the time I laugh. But it's time people got over the jokes, the fears, and the discrimination. Old age isn't catchy. I understand the media is obsessed with youth. Fine. But there isn't anything wrong with getting older. It happens. It's healthy. And it is a reality — our reality. As the ranks of seniors and elderly grow, we should think of it as the new normal — a desirable new normal that does away with ageism and commands respect. How does this happen? I think we may need a revolution. We have gone through the Women's Movement, the Civil Rights Movement, and the Gay Rights

Movement. Why not the Gray Rights Movement?

The Gray Rights Movement has something going for it the others lacked — actually two things: (1) no one is going to get hurt in this revolution — we'll move slow and deliberately: protests will end early so we can be back home before the ten o'clock news; and (2) old age is blind to differences and labels: black, yellow, white, gay, straight, conservative, liberal, Christian, Jewish, atheist, rich, poor, middle class — everyone has a shot at it. And everyone should want it. The number of people sixty-five and older is only getting larger, as is the number of people eighty-five and older. Life is getting longer, which is a good thing if it is done right. How do we do it right?

We have to rewrite the rules, which I am doing at my age, by focusing on living, not dying. I am married to a young woman who finds me charming, fun, and dashing (her words). I perform four-part harmony with a singing group I put together about fifteen years ago as a retirement gift to myself. And if the right scripts come my way, I say, "Yes! When do we start?"

But I'm not an isolated case. There's an eighty-something movie producer up the street from me who drives a Tesla. There are a couple of guys in the neighborhood well past seventy who carry their long boards under their arm every morning as they head out to catch waves. My friends Carl Reiner, Mel Brooks, Richard Sherman, Don Rickles, and Bob Newhart continue to work. Likewise the handful of senior statesmen I only know from TV but see all the time, including politician Bernie Sanders; Bob Schieffer, seventy-seven, the recently retired host of CBS's Sunday talk show *Face the Nation; NBC Nightly News* anchor emeritus Tom Brokaw, seventy-five; and Charlie Rose, who, at seventy-three, seems to work both mornings and nights.

And I don't want to overlook the women, who on average outlive men — and can probably out-work us too. Jane Fonda, seventy-seven, and Lily Tomlin, seventy-four, are starring in a new television series; Betty White is cracking jokes in her nineties; and Supreme Court Justice Ruth Bader Ginsberg is still fighting the good fight as a nimble-minded octogenarian.

Clearly we have entered a new era. As the instigator of the Gray Revolution, I suggest ignoring the anti-aging tips that are so prevalent in the media and search for pro-aging tips. I want to see more older people celebrated for continuing to be vital and active as role models. I want to see experience valued. I want to see older people appreciated in the workforce. I would like to see more people sixty-five and up in movies and on TV in roles other than commercials targeting memory loss, heart disease, diabetes, urinary problems, arthritis, cancer, depression, insomnia, anxiety, high cholesterol, erectile dysfunction, and Crohn's disease.

And put older people behind the camera too. Many of the comedy writers I knew from the sixties and seventies, brilliantly funny, clever people, could not get hired in the eighties and nineties. By the 2000s they were dead. How many laughs did we miss? Speaking of laughter, I once worked with an actress who told me to stop making her laugh; she didn't want to get wrinkles. I'd rather end up a very amused prune than miss a laugh.

I have a feeling that Baby Boomers get this, and they'll rewrite the rules, making the concept of old age as it has been known obsolete. Stereotypes of old people as frail, forgetful, boring, cranky, sick, unattractive, and unproductive will be replaced by pictures of eighty-year-olds scaling mountains, starting new businesses, going back to school, creating great art, discovering new talents and passions, and figuring out new ways to improve life's twilight years.

My hope is this will have a positive impact on the worlds where I have experience: comedy, music, and entertainment. Too much of acting on TV today and comedy more specifically, seems the same, without distinction. Everyone looks the same: there's canned laughter; people get hysterical at a door slamming, and the shows are sped up to cram more into twenty-two minutes. It ruins the timing. My advice to TV producers and writers: let your shows breathe, take a moment, be human, make it real. That's where you find the funny.

I think the same can be said of music. Every time I get in the car and turn on the radio it sounds the same. I don't know one band from the other, but I've been informed that FM radio is playing the same songs that have been played for the past forty years, and that is too bad. It's boring. It misses out on other great music — Duke Ellington, Woody Herman, Art Tatum, Charlie Parker, George Gershwin, Cole Porter. Mix it all together.

I do. We started singing "All About That Bass" at a Vantastix rehearsal. It was a pretty good tune — and I liked its message too.

Life is about variety, and music has always

been my road to it. At seventeen, I was a DJ at the local radio station in my hometown, Danville, Illinois, and I played the same records over and over again. I quickly lost my taste for the popular music and began to explore new bands. Through Stan Kenton and his orchestra, for instance, I discovered saxophonist Stan Getz and singer Anita O'Day. I also remember perking up when I heard the Sauter-Finegan Orchestra, a pretty adventurous group in their day. Glenn Gould's recording of Bach's "Goldberg Variations" remains as fresh and exciting to me as it did when I first heard it in the 1950s. I also loved Sinatra, and I have not seen anyone with the versatility onstage as Sammy Davis Jr.

Once, I saw Lena Horne at the Fairmont in San Francisco, and she took my breath away. I was also a fan of Carmen McRae, one of the greatest jazz singers I ever heard. She just happened to come along at the same time as other greats like Ella Fitzgerald and Sarah Vaughn. I envy young people the thrill of hearing these great artists for the first time.

This whole concept of rewriting the rules is really about being open to discovery and learning and appreciating life — all of life, not just from birth to age sixty-five. Henry

David Thoreau's great quote, "You must live in the present, launch yourself on every wave, find your eternity in each moment . . . there is no other life but this" is even more meaningful later in life, when you know your time is limited.

Back in the midsixties I was made an elder in the Presbyterian church where I took my family. I used to speak on Laymen's Sundays, as they were called, and my talks became fairly popular. Suddenly I found myself on the circuit, driving out to towns and speaking on Sundays. My primary topic was the hypocrisy of people who were pious only one day a week. "What about the other six days?" I used to ask.

Though popular, my turn as a speaker didn't last long — my heart wasn't in it.

And then I lost my taste for organized religion. After the Watts Riots, race, and, more specifically, racism within the Los Angeles Police Department made it to the top of the news, similar to what has happened recently in Baltimore, Ferguson, and Cleveland, a number of us at our church felt like we should do something to try to heal the city and understand the issues. Someone suggested inviting a Baptist choir from Watts to our church. I thought that was a great idea. What better place than a church to bring people together? What better place to celebrate differences and discover similarities? And how perfect to do that with music?

But in a meeting of the church elders several people objected. They did not want any black people in the church. I was disgusted. I left that meeting, and that was my last Sunday in any church.

I wasn't quite done with religion, though. I began attending Jewish services with the Congregation Beth Ohr, whose members met in a Unitarian church in Studio City. Anybody was welcome. I was impressed with their rabbi, a man named Michael Roth. He would speak for thirty minutes, and then everybody went in another room, had coffee and cake, and discussed the service. They questioned ideas, debated them, related them to the real world, and talked about how the age-old themes might be applied to our lives. To me, that felt more like it.

I attended services for about six months and then lost touch with the rabbi until not too long ago when our paths happened to cross. He was in his nineties.

"What do you do now?" I asked.

"I'm still learning," he said. "Still reading and learning."

Letters to an Editor

DIAGNOSIS MURDER
Viacom Productions
7700 Balboa Blvd.
Van Nuys, CA 91406

DICK   VAN   DYKE

Brian Lowry
L.A. Times
Times Mirror Square
Los Angeles, CA 90053

30 November 1999

Dear Mr. Lowry,

I have come to the conclusion that you have it in for us
old folks. You referred to our TV series as "Geezer TV."
Now you suggest we have a quiz show and award Viagra as

Let me say first that I am 74 years old, and I think I can whip your ass.

Growing old is not a lepper colony where an unfortunate few are sent to die. It is a precious gift given only to some lucky human beings. Sad to say, it's not an award of merit. Even you might live to experience it, if somebody doesn't do you in first.

I hope you live long enough to acquire the insight, wisdom, and understanding that comes with growing "old."

Warm regards,

DICK VAN DYKE

DVD:st

Viacom Productions, Inc., A Viacom International Company
10880 Wilshire Blvd., Suite 1101, Los Angeles, CA 90024,

Dick Van Dyke
c/o Diagnosis Murder
Viacom Productions
7700 Balboa Blvd.
Van Nuys, CA 91406

Dear Mr. Van Dyke:

I greatly appreciated your note and would love to find some
way to showcase your views in the Los Angeles Times. Here are
the three most likely options:

A) I would be happy to interview you about perceived agism in
the media for a follow-up column.

B) You could write a "Counterpunch" column yourself
expanding on the points you made.

C) We could publish your letter, which I wouldn't do without
your permission.

I would like to offer a few disclaimers. For starters, I didn't write the "geezer" line (that was my colleague, Paul Brownfield), and I actually have championed opportunities for older writers and performers, including a recent interview with Barney Rosenzweig and a column about the many veteran actors responsible for the success of popular series.

That said, given the emphasis on adults 18 to 49 at the networks, and the audience profile of your program, it's hard not to make a crack at its expense now and again.

Feel free to call me regarding which of the options you prefer. I look forward to hearing from you.

Best,

Brian Lowry

Brian Lowry

P.S. My mother, 76, says I am very kind to old people, though I suspect she, too, could whip my ass.

OLD THINGS — AND WHAT REALLY MATTERS

No one was more surprised than me to hear that the striped satin blazer I wore in the "Jolly Holiday" scene in *Mary Poppins,* the one where Bert the chimney sweep dances with animated penguins, sold at auction. According to reports, a collector of movie memorabilia paid over $60,000 for it. The label still had my name on it. As far as I know, that was the second time the jacket was auctioned, and my reaction this time was the same as the last time — wow!

Around the same time, my wife bought a "Dick Van Dyke" signature cardigan that was manufactured at the height of *The Dick Van Dyke Show* in the early 1960s. She's constantly finding rare photos and merchandise of mine on the Internet, and this signature sweater was the latest. She purchased it for $15 and gave it to me as a birthday present. I was pleased to see that the gray sweater had held up over the years.

It had a small fray on one of the sleeves; otherwise all of its original buttons were intact, and it looked pretty good — kind of like me, I suppose.

It's a funny thing, though, about things. I have never felt an attachment to material things. Not old things. Not new things. Not anything. Once I was able to afford sports cars, I went through my share. I owned Corvettes, Jaguars, an Avanti, and even an Excalibur. I enjoyed nice cars. But I didn't "collect" them or anything else. Not stamps or coins or baseball cards. Not ashtrays, matches, or postcards. Not paintings, records, or movies. Not favorite old T-shirts. And obviously not jackets, costumes, or sweaters with my name on the label.

I once read that collecting things is related to anxiety. I am not an anxious person. Is there a connection? I don't worry. I don't get nervous. I can't remember the last time something wound me up. The shelves in my home do not boast anything I would show off to visitors. My parents did not collect anything either. Of course, they didn't have any money. Even if they had been well off, I don't think they would have bothered. They weren't sentimental in that way, and neither am I.

My biggest indulgence over the years has

been clothes. Though I knock around the house in a T-shirt and sweat pants, I like nice, fashionable clothes, a preference I attribute to my father. He loved to dress stylishly. He copied Fred Astaire. He used a necktie in place of a belt and wore ascots. His suits cost $40, which was a good deal but still expensive in the thirties and forties. Like my dad, I also admired Fred Astaire, but I took my fashion cues from Cary Grant. Once I got to New York and had a steady paycheck, I had suits custom made at J. Press. I paid between $200 and $250, probably the equivalent of $2,500 today, but I loved a suit that fit.

It was noticed. I wore my own suits while starring in *Bye Bye Birdie* on Broadway, and I won the After Six Award as "Broadway's best dressed star of the 1960–1961 season." Soon after, following a Friday night performance, there was a knock on my dressing room door. I opened it, and there stood Cary Grant, the most dapper man on the planet. After a congratulatory handshake, he playfully shoved me aside and started going through my suits. "The best dressed star on Broadway? Well, I'll see about that." It tickled me to death.

Today my After Six Award is on a shelf, framed, with a torn piece of paper inside the glass that says, "Well!" and it's signed, "Cary Grant."

Arlene recently unearthed my best-dressed proclamation from a box of stuff I was not aware I had in my possession until she brought it into the house and put it in front of me. She found other boxes too. I didn't know I had three-quarters of the things she pulled from them: a drawing I did of Morey Amsterdam on the set of *The Dick Van Dyke Show,* sketches I did of people on the set of *Mary Poppins,* drawings someone did of me. There were also photos, letters, and more. All great stuff, and each one brought back a warm memory, which is what I really treasured — the memories of having been there in the first place.

My first wife, Margie, deserves all the credit for preserving that memorabilia. She packed all those boxes forty or fifty years ago. If left to me, I am sure it all would have been lost or forgotten. But don't think I'm unsentimental. If you were to walk through my house, you'd see family photos on tabletops and a beautiful landscape on the dining room wall that was painted by my grandson Wes, a terrific artist who still paints on the easel we bought him when he was a kid.

It doesn't take much prompting to get an

update on the other grandchildren: Taryn and Kristen both work with autistic children, Ryan is a talented musician and sound engineer, Tyler just graduated from film school, brothers Carey Wayne and Shane make movies, and Jessica, an extraordinarily bright girl who died tragically of Reye's syndrome when she was thirteen, smiles at all of us from high above.

As for the glitzy Hollywood stuff, it's there, but you have to look up on the bookshelves to see my awards: Emmys, a Grammy, a Tony, and a recent Screen Actors Guild Life Achievement Award. Then there's the statue I cherish most, a one-of-a-kind Chimney Sweep Award that the crew from *Mary Poppins* made for me. I appreciate everything those represent.

But these days I get just as excited about new tools, a set of paints, or a new computer animation program. I also go all-out during Halloween; my garage is full of decorations and devices that make young trick-or-treaters shriek and smile, and I love when I discover a new one.

I guess what I'm saying is that I'm practical minded and like things that entertain my imagination more than the stuff typically coveted for status. Here's why.

About ten years into my first marriage we

moved to a two-hundred-acre ranch in Cave Creek, Arizona, an area north of Scottsdale. Today Cave Creek is fully developed, with homes and shopping malls, but back then it was empty desert almost as far as you could see. Our house was in the middle of nowhere. A creek ran past on one side, and the other side was a wall of sandstone cliffs. The entire mesa, nearly as far as I could see, was part of the ranch. I used to ride a minibike straight across the rugged landscape when I needed to touch base with civilization.

One day when we were hiking, one of my kids spotted a shiny rock. A few minutes later we unearthed an ax head. The digging commenced then and there. The whole family got into it. We noticed partially exposed rocks that were pretty geometric; they turned out to be pottery. Over several years we dug down about five feet until we uncovered an entire village. In 1982 my wife wrote a scholarly book about the structures we excavated and the artifacts we found, gobs of pottery and utensils, tools that were key to everyday life of a tribe of Hohokam Indians who lived on our ranch around 675–850 CE. Or, I suppose, we lived on top of their village about a thousand years later.

Think about that — one thousand years later.

Up until then I thought I owned that land. But the dig set me straight, as did all the stuff that we found. If anyone needed proof of the old adage "You can't take it with you," there it was. We were finding things that had been essential to the Hohokam people's survival. I wondered whether some of them had wanted larger pots or admired their neighbor's ax blades more than their own. Had some of them complained to the chief about living in a ground-floor dwelling, preferring instead a perch higher up the mesa wall, a room with a view? Was it possible they had the same jealousies that plague modern life?

But to what purpose? They disappeared: all their homes, tools, and industry buried under layers of dirt, hidden for an entire millennium until an actor and his family dug them up.

I wondered about their last days. What had happened? There were no volcanoes nearby that would have wiped them out in a single flood of lava. There were no tidal waves. Was it a slow dissipation from desert conditions? Who was left at the end? Ten people? Three? One? Had that last person been so mad they threw the pottery against the wall?

Or had they stacked it all up neatly and walked away?

The site and the thought of a once-vibrant and thriving outpost of humanity quietly disappearing underneath five feet of desert began to give me a perspective on stuff: What helps us survive? What is a waste of time or money? What makes us happy and feel like our lives have meaning? And what really matters?

If that was the start, now, as I near ninety and can look back over many decades of life experiences, joys and heartaches, moves and missed opportunities, seven-inch TVs and sixty-inch TVs, celebrations and disappointments, friendships, separations, reunions, marriages, and divorces, births and deaths, I think I have a handle on the stuff that has truly made a difference, in the deeper sense of giving my life definition and meaning. Not surprisingly, it's also the stuff that continues to do so.

So what do I think really matters?

1. Family and friends: I would hate to think I was alone on this rock floating around the solar system. That's why family and friends matter. Period. I never had a bachelorhood, I suppose. I had planned to marry my high school girlfriend, Nancy

Frankieburger, but she dropped me when I came back from the service. Then I was with Margie for twenty-eight years. I spent thirty-three years with Michelle. Given that track record, I am counting on at least twenty to thirty years with Arlene. I have enjoyed being in relationships and raising a family. For me, life has always been about accepting responsibility for the well-being and happiness of the people I love. Even though I didn't have any money, I embraced the arrival of each one of my children. They give your life gravity and meaning. They create a moral compass that is real, not abstract or theoretical. They have lives of their own, but you can always reel them back in. I'm thinking of the old joke about the couple who find themselves alone on Thanksgiving. The husband calls their children and says, "Your mother and I are getting a divorce." Then he hangs up, turns to his wife, and says, "The kids will be over in fifteen minutes." Friends enjoy a similar standing. They are also people with whom you share your life's experiences. Do they enjoy you? Do you step up when they are in need? Do they want to check in with you? The way we interact with people is what defines us and how we come to be defined. How we spend our time with them is what gives life meaning. You can look in the mirror to see the way you look on the outside. But the way family and friends regard you is a real measure of the way you look on the inside.

2. Questions. Early on, I wanted to feel that my life mattered, that my existence had meaning, and to do so, I had to figure out what mattered to me and then apply myself to it. I knew that I wanted to get into radio, and that led to performing in nightclubs, which opened the door to Broadway and television, and then movies. By that point I was beyond questioning whether I had made the correct choices in my professional life. In terms of my career, I knew I was applying myself the way I was supposed to. But even with success, I heard the constant refrain of my soul asking questions, some of which were within my grasp and others that soared way beyond my reach.

I trace this restless desire to understand the big picture back to my childhood. At eleven, I went to Bible camp. For the next three years, I carried around a Bible which I read from cover to cover. The stories filled me with awe and curiosity, even though my intellectually immature mind strained to understand the meaning within the rich tapestry of allegory. I decided I would become a minister — that is, until I joined the high school drama club.

Suddenly my plans changed. My Bible ended up on the shelf, and I started down the road that eventually landed me in Hollywood. But I never lost my curiosity about my place on this mystical, magical map, nor did I quit asking questions. In fact, success probably made me even more curious about the nature of my existence. I read constantly, mostly theologians and philosophers. Among those whose books I have turned to repeatedly are Søren Kierkegaard, Dietrich Bonhoeffer, and Paul Tournier, a Swiss physician and religious scholar I once met when I wrangled my way into a lunch he and his wife were having with people who brought him to Hollywood.

Though he didn't speak any English, we communicated through an interpreter. I managed to explain that I was impressed with the way he applied his biblical teachings to his patients. In a way I applied my principles to my work, making it a rule long ago not to work on any projects that my children couldn't see.

The thing these writers have in common is that they mostly ask questions, either of themselves or others, but especially of those who claim to know all the answers. Doubt shines through all of their writing, an unrelenting, resilient doubt that I relate to intellectually. As I have grown older and, hopefully, wiser, I've come to see that there are no sure answers, only better questions — questions that get us closer to the truth about whatever it is we want or need to know. Just knowing you don't have the answers, in fact, is a recipe for humility, openness, acceptance, forgiveness, and an eagerness to learn — and those are all good things.

All good things begin with a question. French fries or mashed potatoes? Red or white? Dessert? Chocolate or vanilla? Have you ever been to the Grand Canyon? What about Paris? Do you want the job? Will you marry me? Do you want to try to have a baby? Why am I here? What am I supposed to do while I am here?

In the early 1960s I sat alongside Dr. Martin Luther King Jr. at a rally in Los Angeles. I was there because writer Rod Serling asked a simple question: "Will you help Dr. King?"

At the rally I sloughed off warnings that someone might take a shot at Dr. King. "I'll lean to the left," I joked.

If someone had taken a shot and the bullet had hit me instead, I suppose I would have been okay with dying for a cause like racial equality, though it would have been way too soon for me to go. I would have missed joining the NOH8 campaign for marriage equality, as I did recently. That also began with a question: "Do you believe in equality?" And it involved the converse: "Why do people hate?"

Hate is such a terrible waste of time. I don't think people who hate should receive the attention they seem to garner in the media. Entire cable networks have been created to hate each other. Our political system seems to have devolved into one side hating the other. I like to ask, "Why do you hate?" It is so much easier to help. It's the easiest thing in the world. Help can mean writing a check. It can also mean sharing a smile or saying hello. One time when I was serving food to the homeless at the Midnight Mission in downtown L.A., a man seemingly in his forties recognized me and asked, "Why are you here?" It bothered me that we live in a world where he had to ask. "Why wouldn't I be here?" I said.

It's important to ask questions. Questions matter. Good questions matter even more. If you don't have any questions, here are some to carry around in your pocket:

Why not me?

What can I do to help?

How can you be so sure?

Can I do better this time rather than next time?

What don't I know that I should know?

What do I need to do next so that I don't worry about not having done it?

Do I have everything I need as opposed to everything I want?

Am I using my time productively?

How can I use it better?

Do I like my work? If not, what would I like to do?

What's missing? How can I fix that?

Am I okay with myself? If not, why?

Am I doing better?

How can I help other people do better?

Is my heart open?

Have I said I'm sorry to those who need to hear it?

Have I said I love you to those I want to tell?

3. Music. Why does music matter? In the most personal terms, it gave me a relationship with my father. He didn't understand me, but we liked the same music, and it was always something we could talk about. Music also played a crucial role in my career, starting with my first job as a disc jockey. For as long as I can remember, though, music has been a part of my daily life, whether it was playing with the band in school, singing or dancing to make a living, or playing the piano in the early morning or late at night, as I do nowadays, filling the quiet with chords that give, as Plato said of music, "soul to the universe, wings to the mind, flight to the imagination, and charm and gaiety to life and to everything."

Listen to Bach, Benny Goodman, or Cole Porter, and then try to tell me music doesn't make life more delightful, delicious, and delovely. I know for a fact it does. A few years ago I was singing with my quartet the Vantastix at a children's hospital on the East Coast. We went from room to room, singing songs to groups of kids, roommates, and families. If we found a kid, we sang.

Doctors, nurses, and the kids themselves said the songs were the best medicine they had received, adding fun to the otherwise dreary and depressing routine of their hospital stay. The last room we entered was nearly dark, with just a small shaft of light sneaking in behind the drawn shades. A boy who looked to be about fourteen years old was lying on top of the bed, a single IV attached to his arm. He was painfully thin and bald. His eyes were closed. He was obviously very sick. Even though it seemed as if we might be disturbing him, the nurse who led us into his room nodded that it was okay to sing. We did a couple of songs, singing very softly, our voices careful to soothe and not disturb. He didn't respond, didn't open his eyes, and didn't stir until we finished and started to tiptoe out. Then we heard a quiet voice, barely a whisper, say, "Would you please sing another one?" That alone is why music matters.

4. Books. I love ideas and stories. I always have at least one book going and am on the lookout for the next one. They feed the brain and fuel the imagination. I can't imagine life without them. As a kid, I read all the way through Edgar Rice Burroughs's Tarzan books. I liked *King Arthur and the Knights of the Round Table,* and of course, I loved Mark Twain. Booth Tarkington was another writer I liked when I was growing up. He wrote the Penrod series, *Penrod and Sam* and the two other books in the trilogy about the adventures of a twelve-year-old boy. I identified with those stories.

I also enjoyed stories about the Civil War and sea adventures. I used to have dime novels. They were printed on rough paper and only cost a dime, but some of the writers were among the greats, such as Ray Bradbury and Isaac Asimov. Only a dime — that's how much it cost to time travel. Can you imagine? I read those books by the handful. The collection I had as a kid is the one thing I wish I still had. In fact, the only thing I have saved from my childhood is my copy of *King Arthur*. It wasn't deliberate. It seems to have followed me around. But I am glad to have it.

5. A sense of humor. I once heard someone say that if you can't laugh at life, you're missing the joke. I agree. As far as I'm concerned, a sense of humor is the way we make sense out of nonsense.

A SEPARATE PLOT

There was a young man from Dallas
who overdosed on Cialis.
His body was laid
to rest in the shade
with a separate plot
for his phallus.

I WAS SUPPOSED TO GO FIRST

We spoke about it a handful of times, none that stand out for any particular reason. We did not dwell on it either. As far as I was concerned, I was being practical and preparing my longtime partner, Michelle, a woman of deep and wild dispositions, for what seemed inevitable: that I was likely to die first.

I did not want to die, obviously. But I was six years older than Michelle, and it made sense to me that I would go before her. Starting in childhood, we are programmed to believe the oldest ones are supposed to go first. It's the natural order of things. It doesn't always happen that way, of course. Many factors come into play, such as smoking, genetics, luck. But it's a waste of time trying to cover all those variables. I focused on the statistics. I was older, and women generally outlive men. I think the average expectancy these days for women is eighty-one, compared to seventy-six for men. This is actually good news for survival of the species. In an evolutionary sense, women are more essential than men. In a practical sense, they make plans, write thank-you notes, and remember birthdays.

Bottom line: I was going before Michelle. Up the ladder to some unspecified rung, then . . . adios.

We were never maudlin about it. Saying "good-bye" when I left for work or ran out to the grocery store did not take on additional weight. In fact, we only had the conversation a few times before folding it up and putting it in the back of the underwear drawer. Things were understood. Beyond making sure she was provided for, I had only one concern about her quality of life without me, and I was very clear to her about it. I did not want my death to turn her into a professional widow. I didn't want her to spend the rest of her life grieving. I didn't even want her to mourn for a year, which is supposed to be the respectfully appropriate time to wait. I wanted her to fall in love again. I wanted this woman who was a rare force of passion and humor, a powerhouse of pure energy, to continue to live life to the fullest.

"Make sure you get on with your life," I said.

Michelle worked as my agent's assistant at the William Morris Agency when we met in the early 1970s. I would call to speak with him and found myself chatting with her until he was available. Pretty soon I was calling just to talk with her. At the time Michelle, a former singer and actress, was embroiled in a "palimony" lawsuit against her former companion, actor Lee Marvin, whom she met when she got a small part in his 1964 movie *Ship of Fools*. They lived together for six years.

After breaking up in 1970, he sent her a small monthly sum, reportedly to help get her back on her feet. But when those checks stopped, she filed suit for half of the money he had earned while they were together. Her lawyer called it palimony, and every media outlet in the country followed it. Although the lawsuit was a landmark case, it created a notoriety that overwhelmed Michelle. The legal battle also saddled her with significant additional expenses, as she employed a very expensive attorney, Marvin Mitchelson.

We started living together in 1978. A year later her lawsuit went to trial. Media coverage ran the gamut from the *New York Times* to the *National Enquirer* and prompted fierce debate on the obligations of men and women who enter into relationships without marrying. Michelle stood tall and strong throughout the public ordeal — not surprising to anyone who knew her. After ultimately losing the case, she famously told reporters, "If a man wants to leave his toothbrush at my house, he better bloody well marry me."

And that's what I wanted to do from the first day Michelle moved into my place in Marina del Rey. We got along perfectly. We ate and drank, took long walks, and went to movies and parties. She made me more social. In turn, I took her on adventures aboard my sailboat, which was like a second home. I was a confident skipper in those days, and she was an enthusiastic passenger who was quite clear that, with a cigarette in one hand and a cocktail in the other, she was more than occupied and not interested in learning the skills that would have elevated her to capable first mate.

Once, in one of our more memorable adventures, we flew to the British Virgin Islands, where I rented a forty-foot sailboat. We threw some groceries on it and took off for two weeks, sailing wherever our whims and the wind took us. Though I knew it was futile, I was still trying to teach her the basics of sailing, especially how to anchor. After all, we were on our own.

"Keep it into the wind while I drop anchor," I remember saying.

She gave me one of those looks that said, "Yeah, yeah, yeah." Then one day we were out, and the wind was blowing hard, about forty knots. I was up front getting the anchor and lowering the sail while Michelle had hold of the steering wheel. In those conditions, though, I was having trouble, in part because of the wind but mostly because Michelle was steering us in circles.

"Starboard!" I yelled. "Starboard! Take us starboard!"

She looked directly at me, shaking her head. I wasn't sure whether she couldn't hear me or didn't understand. I was focused on the tedious job at hand: the lines and sail were wrapped around the mast. I needed help. I issued another command, "Starboard!" and looked directly at my first mate to see whether she could hear me.

Michelle heard me all right. She snapped, "Don't give me that Navy crap! Just say right or left!"

When we moved to Malibu from the Marina in 1990, I discovered something new and wonderful about Michelle. She had a green thumb. It wasn't just green; it was the greenest thumb I had ever encountered. Whatever she planted in our backyard — a big, sloping hill — or in one of the many flower beds seemed to grow and bloom. Sometimes she tossed seeds willy-nilly or took cuttings from plants she saw along the road when we were walking, and they always grew.

She spent hours outside planting and pruning. The gardens she created were glorious, and they still are. The yard continues to bloom year-round. She left her green thumbprint everywhere. The animals and the insects, the birds and the bees appear to appreciate the plants and flowers as much as I do, if not more. It is a testimony to the impact we humans have on the earth — our little patch of dirt or the big blue orb itself. We can destroy it, or we can make it even better than we found it. Michelle definitely made it better.

She had a similarly positive effect with people. She was a strong, aggressive woman, and I liked her because of this. She was also a fiercely loyal friend. If she was your friend, you could count on her for anything, and people did. She knew everyone and introduced me to a world of new people, from Dick Martin and his wife, Dolly, to Barbara Sinatra and so many others who became my close friends. I was lucky she dragged me along. It was this large, closely knit social circle of hers that provided comfort whenever I thought about her going on without me.

"There will be no sitting around in the dark," I said. "No wasting time. No waiting a year before resuming life — and hopefully love."

She nodded, and I knew she would take care of things in my absence and that people would take care of her. I would have left her comfortable too. That was also paramount in my thoughts. Like a good Boy Scout, my campsite would be cleaned and tended to when I left, which was important to my peace of mind. My loved ones wouldn't have to worry. In those private moments when I did my estate planning and thinking, and just thinking minus the estate planning, I wanted to know my exit would be on favorable terms.

I am not saying it wouldn't be sad. But there would be no sense that I had dined and dashed. Maybe I wouldn't have sung all the songs I wanted to sing, but I wouldn't have missed many, and just as importantly, because life wasn't all about me, the bills would be paid, my slippers put in their place, and everyone told they were loved.

The thing neither of us anticipated or even considered was that Michelle might go before me. We ignored that she didn't take care of herself. She drank, smoked, and was overweight. She treated life as if it were a party. Sometimes she was the guest. Other times she was the hostess. And other times she was the headliner, belting out a couple of tunes. She enjoyed herself.

One afternoon, back when I was still shooting *Diagnosis Murder,* she was picking up some samples at a clothing manufacturer. She felt fine. On her way out, though with her arms full of clothes, she hopped over a low fence in an effort to get to her car quicker and felt a sharp pain in her chest, so sharp that she lost her breath. She didn't know what was happening. She drove to the CBS studio where I was working on a new show and found me on the set.

I took one look at her — she had literally turned purple — knew she was in trouble, and got her to lie down in my dressing room while we called an ambulance. Within minutes, she was being rushed to the hospital, where doctors determined that she'd had a heart attack. Michelle understood, yet she still wanted to leave the hospital immediately, and she put up quite a fuss. It was just her personality. In the end, she listened to the doctors and stayed close to a week, and the most remarkable thing happened to her while she was there: she quit smoking.

None of us could believe it, including her. Michelle was a chain-smoker, one of the last and one of the worst. She used to smoke in the shower — that's how bad her habit was. At one time I had been a heavy smoker, but I had quit and tried to get her to quit too. She never could until that stint in the hospital, after which she swore that the Jamaican nurse who took care of her did something to her — Michelle called it healing voodoo — because she checked out of the hospital and never wanted a cigarette again. I figured we had dodged a bullet. Even after the heart attack I still imagined myself leaving her a widow. She did too.

As Michelle bounced back, my first wife, Margie, was diagnosed with cancer. I made sure she had the best care, and in 2008, after a tough battle, she passed away.

By then Michelle was engaged in her own fight with the Big C. In the spring a nagging cough took her into the doctor, who found a spot on her lung. Long story short: they ended up taking out the whole upper half of her lung, followed by the usual unpleasant but necessary stuff, chemo and radiation.

As an unshakable optimist, I thought she was going to beat the disease. It wasn't going to be easy, but Michelle had the best doctors in the city and a spirit that was like a buoy in the open sea. No matter how large a wave crashed down, she popped back up. Radiation treatments were five days a week. After that we went to chemo, where I kept her company while she was on the drip. I ate sandwiches they brought around and watched TV. We followed directions and prayed. But her cancer metastasized anyway.

Few words convey the sadness and helplessness of saying good-bye to someone you love, someone with whom you've shared every day for thirty-one years, as I had with Michelle. I remembered thinking back to the first time we met with her oncologist. Michelle asked, "Is there anything I can do?"

"Well, you ought to be on the safe side," he said. "It's probably a good idea to get your affairs in order."

She never did get her affairs in order, nor did she ever marry me. How ironic is that? We had our own agreement, of course, but I wanted to get married for legal reasons and all the other reasons that kept us together for three decades.

"Let me count the ways," as Elizabeth Barrett Browning wrote. She knew it too, but she always put it off, with a throaty laugh. Then it was too late, and I found myself listening to her say the things I had always told her: "I don't want you to go through the obligatory year of mourning. . . . Life is too short. . . . Don't waste time. . . . I love you."

I used to ask people, "Of all the things you enjoyed doing during your life and can't do anymore, what do you miss most?" I had asked Michelle long before she got sick, and she said, "Having lunch with the girls." Of course, she still could have had lunch with the girls, and she did go out with her friends, but I knew what she meant. She was talking about being young, twentysomething, when she went out with the girls, and all of life and its possibilities were still ahead of her. It's a wonderful memory, a feeling that is worthy of a wistful smile and a faraway, dreamy look.

Attitude. So much of life is about attitude — or, more accurately, having a good attitude. In terms of the death of friends and loved ones, attitude takes a backseat to being practical, to opening your heart and being practical about the fact that everyone lives and dies, and although we don't get to choose the way we die, we do have a big say in the way we live.

I also think belief is crucial. I believe in a Higher Power, whatever that means. It means something different to different people. I don't think anyone can claim with absolute certainty to know what that means, only that there is a Higher Power, one we should respect.

In terms of life, death, and an afterlife, I am a great admirer of author Norman Cousins, who suggested that upon death or after death, your soul probably goes on, but not your physical body. That ceases to exist anymore, and eventually it decays and disappears. Only your spirit survives, and in that realm you don't have any memory of having lived.

I think he's pretty close there, as close as anybody has ever gotten to what happens, which makes the way you live even more important. It is the only time you have to recall and assess and account for those experiences, the connections you had with other people, the work you did, the words you said, and the friends and family you leave behind. So it's worth making sure those scrapbooks are filled. Make sure you have fun. Make sure you smile and laugh. Make sure you live.

Here's a final note about Michelle: she spent her last morning alive on the telephone, talking with her friends. At noon she went into a coma — and that was it. The last thing she ever said to me was, "You made me a better person."

Then it was just me and our dog, Rocky, and all of Michelle's things in the house, which suddenly felt very large and empty. It was October 2009, the day before Halloween, in fact. I remember going outside to put the finishing touches on my annual Halloween decorations, for which I was renowned in our neighborhood; I had contemplated taking the year off, but Michelle had insisted I go on with the show. I could hear her voice as I worked. The weather was still warm, and the yard was still green and the gardens in bloom. It was beautiful. It was all Michelle's doing.

But I couldn't help thinking that I was supposed to go first.

I would like to say a few words in tribute to a cricket who lives in my garden. Unlike the hundreds we had when we first moved here, he was the only one who showed up this year. He sings his little heart out, trying to make it sound like a summer night. It's sad. My heart goes out to him, as it does to the Mariposa butterfly who flits madly around the flowers, trying to pretend it's the annual invasion of former years. There is one dragonfly who has thrown in the towel, I think. He makes a couple of passes over the pool in the morning, but then we don't see him anymore. We have three flies in the kitchen who do a pretty good job of pestering my wife.

I found a nice environmental CD of rain on the roof. We were using it to get to sleep at night, but the neighbors complained we were running our sprinklers too late.

We had a bee early in June. But he fell in the pool and drowned. Wouldn't it be funny if next spring we weren't here either?

*I wrote this ditty one afternoon in 2008.

SIT OR GET OFF THE POT ROAST

As near as I can figure, the history of the pot roast is as plain and basic as the ingredients themselves. It seems to have originated on farms in the 1800s where the cooking was done in large pots dangling over a hearth. A big slab of meat and an assortment of vegetables were tossed in, and everything cooked slowly in natural juice, water, wine, or some kind of stock. Recipes began to appear in cookbooks at the end of the 1800s.

By the early 1900s pot roast was standard fare in homes across America. The 1904 edition of *The Modern Cook Book and Household Recipes* included a recipe for "Braised Beef Pot Roast"; a similar recipe appeared in the 1937 version of *My New Better Homes and Gardens Cook Book*. And when André Simon described the roasting of a two-and-a-half-pound rump of beef in his 1952 book, *A Concise Encyclopedia of*

Gastronomy, the pot roast was referred to as "an old Yankee recipe."

I mention this only because, while doing my research, I did not find instructions anywhere that a pot roast should be delivered weekly to someone who has lost their spouse. But as soon as word got out that Michelle was gone, my family and friends showed their concern by dropping off food. One day I came home and found a large pan of meatloaf on the front porch. Another time it was a baking dish of lasagna. Then someone brought a pot roast. Some dishes were delivered with reheating instructions; others came with a loving note, "Call if you need anything else." Pretty soon what I needed was more freezer space to store the food.

I like pot roast, meatloaf, and lasagna as much as anyone, maybe even more. As my wife, Arlene, has learned, my taste in food was shaped during my midwestern youth. My favorite meal, for instance, is fried chicken, corn on the cob, and mashed potatoes, followed closely by meatloaf, pot roast, and lasagna. I have never tired of any of these dishes.

But the casseroles friends dropped off and the messages they left, "Dick, it's me — and I want to come by with some food," took on a momentum that I couldn't keep up with. I could only eat so much, and my appetite had disappeared.

Then I realized that the pot roasts were more than considerate goodwill gestures, more than mere precooked meals I could pull out of the refrigerator when I got hungry, more than a favorite recipe intended to help out until I got back into a routine. They were coded messages!

It was as clear as the mozzarella on top of the lasagnas. All these meals were dropped off by women who were also single, many of them widowed themselves; they were letting me know they were out there — and available. It was as if a secret message had been sent to every widowed female of a certain age from Malibu to Beverly Hills: *Girls, we have a live one. He's eighty-three, he's got all his marbles, and he can still dance. Perfect for the charity circuit. Get your pot roasts ready.*

At the gathering that followed Michelle's service I had jokingly asked all the rich widows to move to one side, a light moment that drew laughter from everyone. But I wasn't ready for a new relationship. Not then. Not a month later. Not several months later. Writing in the *New York Times* about his own terminal diagnosis, Dr. Oliver

Sacks, one of my favorite authors, noted, at age eighty-one, that the deaths of friends and loved ones leave wounds that don't heal. "There will be no one like us when we are gone, but then there is no one like anyone else, ever," he wrote. "When people die, they cannot be replaced. They leave holes that cannot be filled."

That's the way I felt after losing Michelle. There had not been anyone like her, ever. Certainly not in my life. She had been such a dominant presence. Even as her health declined, she ran things from her bed. The phone rang. I heard her voice. I heard her booming laugh. She wanted dinner — then nothing. Her absence left a giant-sized hole everywhere I turned. Someone asked how I dealt with the grief. I didn't. I didn't eat well. I forgot to pay bills. I declined invitations to go out. I fell off the track and didn't know how to get back to living my life.

I wasn't alone. Rocky, our wire hair fox terrier, was equally bereft. He searched endlessly for Michelle, and then after a while, he parked himself in front of me with the same look of sadness, loss, and confusion that was on my face. I tossed his toy across the living room, watched him bring it back, and then tossed it again until he grew bored. He might not have understood what had happened to Michelle, but he knew she was gone. I tried to put things in perspective for him.

"At least you don't have a credit card that's been canceled," I said.

That really happened. My card was canceled, and it wasn't for lack of money to pay the bill; it was because I wasn't organized enough to *find* the bill. That was indicative of the way things unraveled. I had to get it together. I wanted to, believe me. I had told myself repeatedly that I did not want to be one of those people who lose a spouse and stop living. I had seen that in others, both men and women, and I never understood why they let their lives change so dramatically. They quit going to shows, they stopped cooking meals for themselves, they slept late, they moved slower, and they turned into virtual shut-ins. Even when they went out, they were closed off. I did not want that to happen to me. I had promised myself it wouldn't. I had promised Michelle it wouldn't. We had promised each other.

But it was easier said than done. I had never been single. As I said, I had a steady girlfriend in high school who dumped me after I got back from the Air Force. Then I got married to Margie. Then I was with Michelle. Then it was just Rocky and me in the house. I found myself apologizing to him. I promised to change.

I said yes when Gregory Peck's wonderful wife, Veronique, invited me to lunch at a restaurant in Beverly Hills and introduced me to a woman she thought I might like. We had a nice time, but she wasn't my cup of tea. The same thing happened with several other friends who tried to set me up.

Then word got out that I was dating, and my popularity skyrocketed. One woman waited for me every morning in my local coffee shop. She was like a well-intentioned stalker with a nice wardrobe. My phone rang constantly.

I went on quite a few dates, actually — only first dates, mind you — but demand for a widower like me, as I discovered, was such that I might still be going on dates if it were not for my wife, Arlene. At the time she was my makeup artist and friend. We had met a few years before at the SAG awards and worked together enough that I felt comfortable going to her for advice. I had to ask someone — I was a novice. I hadn't dated — really dated — since before World War II.

So I would e-mail her a picture of the woman I was meeting and ask her opinion: "What do you think?" Or, "Have you heard of this restaurant?"

At some point I realized that I looked forward to Arlene's responses more than I did the dates. Pretty soon I quit e-mailing her pictures of other women and suggested the two of us get together. I liked talking to her. I liked her personality. I liked her sense of humor. I liked her take on things. I liked her smiles and her eyes. I liked everything about her. Indeed, I liked the feeling — and this came as a pleasant, unsettling surprise — that I liked her and wanted to be around her.

Does that happen in your eighties?

It sure does.

There was just one problem: the difference in our ages: forty-six years. Ten years is not that big an issue once you're in your thirties; a thirty-five-year-old man with a twenty-five-year-old woman is not a big deal. Twenty years is also an understandable choice, whether you're in your sixties or your eighties. My brother is married to a woman in her sixties. No one questioned that gap when he was in his sixties, and now that he's in his eighties, both of them look smart.

But forty-six years was uncharted territory. Though I was quite sure Arlene knew I was smitten with her, I was not blind to the reality: we were nearly two-and-a-half generations apart, which was like being separated by three time zones, the equator, and another language. Or was it? Or was it not that big of a difference?

I went over the pros and cons, making sure the pros outnumbered the cons, and told myself to be cautious, to take any next steps slowly. I knew that, at eighty-three, I was going to be the major beneficiary of socializing with a beautiful woman in her thirties. At the same time, I sensed that Arlene also enjoyed my company. We had worked together. We e-mailed. We talked on the phone. She occasionally came over and made dinner, or I would pick something up, and she checked in on me. It seemed safe to assume that she was thinking about me almost as often as I was thinking about her — and how to move our friendship into a relationship.

As this happened, I began to feel like myself again. I turned the lights on again. I felt a lightness in my step. I looked forward to talking to Arlene. I had things to say. I wasn't isolated or alone or lonely. It was the darnedest thing. After months of floundering, it was so natural, so effortless. Since then people have asked how I got through the tough parts of losing Michelle. The answer? I didn't. What helped me through this tough period was the same thing that helps in any tough situation, the same thing that had brought me luck when I was struggling in New York with a wife and three young kids when I left the TV station where I worked and auditioned for every play on and off Broadway in order to earn extra money: I opened myself up to the world and all its possibilities, and the world responded.

In this particular instance, I opened my heart. I let life back in. I realized that if I wanted Arlene in my life, I simply had to take a risk. The choice was mine. And it was a simple choice: sit or get off the pot roast.

Promo shots taken in
New York in the 1950s
when I was struggling
to find work. Even when
I had very little money,
I liked to dress as if
I did. *Photograph from
author's private collection*

My wife, Arlene, was originally my personal makeup artist. Here we are on the set of a 3-D short called *The Caretaker*. *Photograph by Jim Udell*

American Gothic: at a friend's 1920s-themed wedding on the *Queen Mary*. It was our first public outing together. *Photograph by Oh! Snap Studios*

Newly engaged, Arlene and I enjoy an alfresco performance of the Los Angeles Philharmonic. *Photograph by Laura Gillespie*

My family at granddaughter Kristen McNally Mullin's wedding in July 2011. Left to right, back row: Shane Van Dyke, Wes Van Dyke, Arlene Van Dyke, me, Kristen McNally Mullin, Russell Mullin, Carrie McNally, Kevin McNally, Christine Van Dyke, Chris Van Dyke, Carey Wayne Van Dyke; front row: Taryn Van Dyke, Ryan Breen, Stacy Van Dyke, Mary Van Dyke, Barry Van Dyke. *Photograph by Curtis Dahl*

Cutting the cake at our intimate first wedding ceremony on Leap Day 2012 at the Serra Retreat in Malibu. *Photograph by Matt Hamill*

September 2012: For our second ceremony our friends Frank and Fay Mancuso lent us their beachfront home for a big, blowout "nautical circus." *Photograph by Ryan Williams, Rawtography*

One of my favorite pictures——we look like a couple of screwball detectives in love.
Photograph by Oscar Zagal

My current headshot.
Photograph by Oscar Zagal

Introducing my *Mary Poppins* costar Julie Andrews as she received a Life Achievement Award from the Screen Actors Guild in 2006. *Photograph by Michael Caulfield/WIREIMAGE. com for TNT, a Time Warner Company*

I've always considered myself a song-and-dance man, so to receive my *own* Life Achievement Award from SAG really tickled me. *Photograph by Mark Hill/TNT*

Backstage after I received my SAG award I did my "headless man" trick, to Arlene's genuine surprise—she'd never seen me do it in person. *Photograph by Kirk McCoy/L.A. Times*

I doodle while on the sets of all my projects. Sometimes I even draw in bed—my "doodling studio!" *Photograph by Arlene Silver Van Dyke*

In 2014 Arlene organized a "Jolly Holiday Bazaar" fundraiser for the Serra Retreat and the Midnight Mission, with which I've been involved for twenty years. You could get your picture taken with "St. Dick"! *Photograph by Loretta Wang/The Social Booth Co.*

September 2014: I was bursting with pride when I presented Arlene with a Golden Heart Award from the Midnight Mission. *Photograph courtesy of the Midnight Mission*

One of the high points of a recent trip on Amtrak was the dining car and our wonderful waiter, Zack. I left him a doodle as well as a tip. *Photograph by Arlene Silver Van Dyke*

Carl Reiner and I have been friends for almost sixty years, but when it comes to valuing imagination, creativity, and joyful curiosity, we've never grown up. *Photograph by Andy Gotts*

Marrying Arlene is one of the best things I've ever done! *Photograph by Andy Gotts*

2015: My a cappella singing group, the Vantastix, posed for the NOH8 Campaign for marriage equality. Left to right: Mike Mendyke, Arlene, me, Eric Bradley, Bryan Chadima. *Photograph by Adam Bouska*

What Do You Talk About with Her?

My brother is caught up in a mystery, even though I have explained the answer to him numerous times. The mystery is my three-year marriage to Arlene. Each time Jerry looks at us, he squints his eyes, shakes his head, and asks, "What do you talk about with her?"

He did it when we were eating lunch together recently. We were having a pleasant conversation about something we both had seen on television, when suddenly he looked up from his cake, shook his head in the direction of Arlene, and asked the question.

I am aware he is asking much more than that singular question, and he probably isn't even interested in the specifics of our conversations, which are obvious to anyone who is around us for more than thirty minutes. In reality, Jerry is saying, "My God, you were already in your forties when she was born. What could you possibly have

147

in common? What are you doing with her? What is she doing with you?"

It's all those questions and more, even if it comes in the form of, "What do you talk about with her?"

I could have asked my brother, "What does anyone talk about with their mate?" relationships being a mystery, and love being the ultimate in the unexplainable. As Albert Einstein mused, "Put your hand on a stove for a minute and it seems like an hour. Sit with that special girl for an hour and it seems like a minute. That's relativity."

Even Friedrich Nietzsche said, "It is not a lack of love, but a lack of friendship that makes unhappy marriages." Arlene and I fell into friendship with ease, and the next steps all seemed natural.

One afternoon, several months into our new friendship-slash-relationship, Arlene came over and my dog, Rocky, and I greeted her at the door, holding a plate of fresh oatmeal cookies from the local bakery. She came inside, and we talked for a while about her day, then I told her about my day, and then I moved to the piano and we sang some songs together — she has a terrific, lively voice. Time passed, then we talked about where we wanted to have dinner, and then I proposed. Marriage.

She rolled her eyes and laughed. It wasn't the first time I had proposed, nor was it the last, but, as she could see from my reaction, it was the most serious I had been up till that point, and suddenly she realized my offer was less of a joke and something I wanted her to consider seriously.

I was new at this, I explained. Having been with one woman for thirty-three years and another for thirty-one years, I was not in the habit of asking women to marry me. Of course, she already knew that about me, along with the fact that I was different from all of the other guys she had dated previously.

We met at the 2006 Screen Actors Guild Awards, where I was introducing Julie Andrews, who was receiving that year's Life Achievement Award. I was backstage, in the artists' green room, talking with Cate Blanchett, when I noticed Arlene. She walked by and sat on a sofa. Something about her caught my eye. I excused myself from Cate and sat down beside Arlene.

"Hi, I'm Dick," I said, beginning what turned out to be a nice, easy conversation. It was strange; something about her simply compelled me to get to know her. In retrospect, it was as if we were supposed to know each other — and there was lots of catching up to do.

"Weren't you in *Mary Poppins*?" she asked before admitting that she had not seen the movie but had recently walked by the El Capitan Theatre on Hollywood Boulevard where it was showing to commemorate the fiftieth anniversary of its release.

I said, "Yes, I was," and told her that the movie was pretty good.

"I guess I should see it," she laughed.

Arlene was a makeup artist and taught at a nearby makeup school. She was friendly and easy to talk to. We chatted until a production assistant came for me. I told Arlene to save my seat. She didn't think I'd return, she later told me, but I did, only to find the cast of *The Mary Tyler Moore Show* had decamped on the sofa.

I introduced Arlene to Valerie Harper. "Are you friends?" Valerie asked.

"It seems like it," I said. "But we just met."

Before I went onstage I asked Arlene for a card. She found one — it was her last one — in her bag. I put it in my tuxedo pocket and promised to call. A few months later, I was getting ready to shoot the made-for-TV movie *Murder 101,* and my regular makeup artist from *Diagnosis Murder,* Stacy Halax, was working on *Desperate Housewives.* I needed someone I liked and trusted. I called and offered the job to Arlene.

She accepted but then had second thoughts after speaking with Stacy, who made the job sound not difficult but . . . delicate.

"Don't talk to him, because everyone talks to him," she told Arlene. "He's too nice and never says no to anyone, and it wears him out. He also needs eye drops. He likes his hair done a certain way. Oh, and work fast. He doesn't like to sit in the chair for more than five minutes."

On Arlene's first day on the set Stacy actually came and watched her airbrush my makeup on to ensure she was doing it correctly. However, once it was clear that Arlene was a pro, everyone relaxed, including her. She understood that Stacy was just being protective.

Even then, I was still easier-going than she had anticipated. I came into the makeup room singing a song and continued singing while she applied the makeup. Arlene sensed that I wasn't in a hurry to leave, and she was right. I was glad to see her. She had a good, positive, capable, and yet relaxed presence.

A few days into the five-week shoot I poked my head out of my trailer at lunchtime and saw Arlene eating with some of the crew at a table outdoors. We were on location, and it was hot outside. I thought she would be more comfortable eating in an air-conditioned room and not having to swat at flies as she ate. Plus, selfishly, I felt like company. So I invited her to have lunch with me in my trailer.

"Sure, thank you," she said with a smile, but as she later confessed, inside she thought, "Oh no, here we go. He's going to hit on me, and this friendship of ours is going to be over."

But it was just lunch and friendly conversation, and after that we ate together regularly. Actually she ate and I watched. For some reason, I was too nervous to eat in front of her. Then one day I suggested eating outside.

"It probably looks bad," I said, "you coming in here all the time."

Arlene appreciated the gesture. But when she saw me sweating through my makeup and swatting at flies, she said, "Let's go back in the trailer." When I was outside and in front of the camera, though, I kept track of her whereabouts and well-being. Once, as I shot a scene, I noticed her sunglasses fall out of her fanny pack. "Did you find them?" I asked afterward. She was dumbfounded.

"Weren't you working? What were you doing looking at me?" Another time I saw the portable chair she was sitting in start to wobble. I stepped away from the camera and found her a sturdier perch. "That's going to be more comfortable," I said.

After the movie we saw each other occasionally when I needed makeup for one of the little jobs I picked up, but I put my career on hold after Michelle began her battle with lung cancer. I told Arlene about the bad news in an e-mail, and she checked in periodically to see how I was doing. It was hard for me to talk about the ordeal, but I liked knowing Arlene was there if I needed to or just wanted to send a note. After Michelle died, Arlene offered condolences, and we e-mailed every so often, but again, she kept a respectful distance. If only she had known how much I wanted to hear from her.

Then one day I received an e-mail from her in which she mentioned that she had taken a job in the art department at a magazine in Woodland Hills, about thirty minutes north of Malibu, and occasionally she drove to the beach on her lunch break to relax. I invited her to visit me anytime she felt like it.

A week or two later she stopped by. It was

the highlight of my day. After that she began stopping by every couple of weeks to fix dinner (usually spaghetti and meat sauce), or else I would pick up something from a local Italian restaurant. As she worked in the kitchen, I would sit on a stool next to the center island and watch her. Later she said she'd noticed my hands were trembling and feared I was developing Parkinson's disease. I wasn't — I was nervous. As our dinners together became more frequent, our talks grew more personal, and a deeper friendship blossomed.

I let her know that I was nuts about her. Still, because of our age difference, I didn't think anything would happen.

Arlene was flattered by my feelings, and deep down she knew she was falling for me too, which blew her mind. As she later told me, she said to herself, "God, there's no way."

But there was a way. It was the thing that kept us calling and seeing each other: we made each other happy.

In late summer 2010 Arlene took a belly dancing class, and when they had a recital a few months later at a small Mediterranean restaurant, I made sure I was in the audience. But we kept our relationship under wraps.

When Arlene's mother, who sat next to me, asked her daughter why I was there, Arlene merely said, "Oh, he's a friend." In September the friendship turned romantic, and we went on our first formal date, to the Magic Castle, a nightclub for magicians in Hollywood. The next month Arlene told her friend Lisa that she was "involved" with me and braced herself for a negative reaction.

But her friend was thrilled. "I love it!" she said. "Enjoy!"

At Thanksgiving she decided to tell her mother. She was very nervous and worried about what the reaction would be, to the point where she didn't know how to even initiate the conversation, until her brother's wife pulled her aside and asked, "Are you and Dick dating?"

Arlene paused long enough that the answer was likely obvious, but then she stuttered, "Yes," after which her sister-in-law reached out and gave her a hug. "I think that's great," she said. Luckily for us, her mother had the same reaction, though we softened her up first with a beautiful jeweled brooch.

As for my side of the family, my son, Barry, and a couple of my grandsons had worked on the *Murder* movies with us, so they already knew her. They had watched the relationship develop from the start. Both my daughters, Carrie Beth and Stacy, said essentially the same thing to Arlene: "As long as my dad is happy." My oldest child, Chris, was skeptical, but as a lawyer, he's supposed to look at situations through that lens, and he came around quickly as he got to know Arlene.

The only one unconvinced was my brother, who met Arlene in 2011 when we were rehearsing for a five-night benefit performance of the play *The Sunshine Boys.* The four of us were at the house, Jerry and his wife, Shirley, and me and Arlene. As we went over lines, Jerry periodically turned toward Arlene with a puzzled look on his face.

At the end of the night, as he and Shirley got up to leave, he gave me one last look, then turned to me and said, "What's going on here?" I didn't respond. I didn't have time — Jerry kept talking. "You two are together? How? You're not exactly *hot.*"

Four years later the four of us were in the same room, and Jerry was saying essentially the same thing: "I don't get it."

"We love each other," I explained.

"But what do you talk about with her?"

It struck me as an absurd question. It seemed obvious — so obvious that I started to make a list.

WHAT DO YOU TALK ABOUT WITH YOUR BEST FRIEND?

1. How'd you sleep?
2. Breakfast
3. The weather
4. The news
5. Errands
6. Work
7. The old photos she found in the closet
8. A new movie on TV
9. An old movie on TV
10. A picture I drew
11. Rehearsals with the singing group
12. Picking new songs
13. Lunch
14. What's Rocky barking at?
15. The bird's nest in the tree out back — isn't spring grand!
16. The pleasure of reading since my cataract surgery
17. The surgery I still need in my other eye

I stopped writing. A list was unnecessary. It was a waste of time. Over ten years, Arlene and I have known each other and become friends, without ever an unnatural or awkward pause in our conversation. In fact, we had only grown closer and found more things to talk about. I could have made hundreds of entries, perhaps more, on that list. Who knows, I might still be working on it now.

More important than what we talk about was that Arlene and I both had someone to talk to. I had lost that special person when Michelle died, and luckily I found a new best friend in Arlene. She found that person in me too.

I'm not saying the differences in our ages is something that will work for everyone, but being open to a new relationship will, with the right person. No one wants to be widowed. But it happens — and a loving heart is a horrible thing to waste. The space and silence resulting from not having someone to talk to, from being lonely and isolated, even if you're surrounded by people, is a terribly destructive, depressing state of being. The key is to connect with someone. I lucked out — again.

Life together is endlessly interesting and full of small talk and talk about big ideas — all sorts of conversation. Sometimes we sit together in silence. Sometimes all we hear are the birds chirping in the backyard. With the right person, that can be like a conversation too.

My brother is funny. His wife is twenty years younger than him, and they never run out of conversation. Of course, that's mostly because Jerry can't remember anything. *Shirley, what's the name of the restaurant where we ate last weekend? What's the name of the guy I need to call? Shirley, what's that movie I liked last week? Shirley, what's for lunch?*

Hey, it works for them.

But to finally and definitively respond to my brother: What do I talk about with Arlene?

What does anyone talk about with his or her best friend?

We talk about everything.

Everything.

SURPRISES

All afternoon I had the sense that I had forgotten to do something. I couldn't figure out what it was until I wandered out to the pool and saw Arlene in the water, standing in the shallow end, between laps, picking tiny patches of calcium crystals off the tiles just above the water line. Suddenly I thought of what it was: it was about Arlene, of course.

I would have asked her right then, but she barely looked up. I got a friendly, "Hey you," and then she was back to business.

She was so focused on chip-chip-chipping away that she didn't notice that a couple of her knuckles were bleeding, never mind that I was standing there with something to ask her. She had been fixated on removing these crystals for the past week, explaining she was addicted to the gratification she felt when she was able to see the original indigo-blue pool tile. I think she was on day five of this obsession. The pool did look beautiful — I had to give her that.

As I recall, it was a gorgeous day. In June 2010 there was a sapphire-blue sky overhead and songbirds in the trees. I thought about how to capture her attention. I started to whistle a tune — that did it.

She looked up with an inviting grin and asked, "Yes?"

At that point if I had been sixty years younger — no, maybe just thirty years younger — I might have dropped down to one knee and said I had something important to ask her.

Instead, I remained upright, poised solidly on two feet but smiling that kind of broad, genuinely happy grin that can only be inspired by a beautiful young woman. I put my hands in my pockets and shifted my weight from one foot to the other.

"Yes?" she repeated.

"I have something to ask you," I said.

Again Arlene asked, "Yes?" only now her smile was larger, amused and interested. Then, for the twelfth or twenty-seventh or sixty-fifth time, I asked her to marry me.

It wasn't a joke, but it had become a sort of through-line of the past year of our relationship. I had popped the question only a couple of nights earlier, in fact, while we watched *Jeopardy* after dinner, and as always, she laughed at me.

It was a laugh filled with love, and though not exactly a rebuff, it was more or less a response that said, "Are you crazy?" Yes, in fact, I was crazy — crazy about her. What is that old saying about the definition of insanity? Doing something over and over again and expecting a different result? Well, I guess I was partially insane. But I was also an adherent of the old English proverb about perseverance.

'Tis a lesson you should heed:
Try, try, try again.
If at first you don't succeed,
Try, try, try again.

So I had tried again — and this time, after I asked, she looked up from the pool and said, "Where's the ring?"

"Do you want to go to Tiffany's today?" I asked.

She smiled. "Okay."

The reason Arlene finally said yes? As she later explained, despite her fears about our age difference and worries that a marriage as far-fetched as ours would never work, her gut told her to take the risk. Stranger things happened to people. Plus, her feel-

162

ings, like mine, were genuine.

So later that afternoon we walked into Tiffany's on Rodeo Drive in Beverly Hills. Arlene said she felt like Julia Roberts in *Pretty Woman.* I felt even luckier. Another couple was also at the counter picking out a ring. They appeared to be in their early thirties and quite indecisive. The bride-to-be tried on every diamond ring in the case.

By contrast, Arlene, whose knuckles were still tinged with blood, studied the options for a few minutes, then tapped the top of the display case and said, "That one." It was a platinum band with tiny diamonds all the way around. We were out of there within twenty minutes. The other couple was still trying on rings.

Back out on Rodeo Drive I held Arlene's hand and walked with a spring in my step. I was tickled as I thought about what had just happened. I was engaged. Who would have guessed? However, after ninety years on this planet, I can confirm one absolute, fundamental, inarguable truth about life: it is an endless series of surprises. We old people — no, make that us folks who have lived a long time — have learned this basic truth: no one knows what is going to happen next. It's all a mystery wrapped in a gift box that you only find when you least expect it.

Think about it: life starts as a surprise, we spend our childhood pretty much in the moment, and then, after a certain point, we spend a good amount of energy planning for the future, wondering but never actually knowing when, how, or why we will head for the exit. All the years in between are best summed up by that oft-quoted line, which I will say again here: if you want to amuse God, make plans. If anyone who tells you they have everything mapped out, check back with them five years later. You can say, "I told you so."

Philosopher Alan Watts said as much in *The Wisdom of Insecurity,* a favorite book of mine that postulates that security does not exist, not in life and definitely not in the way people want and spend their time trying to ensure it — my younger self included. Watts argued what he called "the wisdom of insecurity." He said that in order to live with less anxiety and a freer mind, you have to accept that insecurity is the rule. The best you could do, he said, was be fully present in the here and now — and get ready to be surprised.

As I always say, my life has been a series of surprises — lucky breaks, I call them — starting with what was and remains one of the best experiences of my life. I was a freshman in junior high, and my dad was transferred in his sales job, from Danville to Crawfordsville, Indiana. We lived across from Wabash College, and on Sundays they had track meets there. I was on my school's freshman track team, and our coach was one of the officials at those weekend events. I always went over and watched the races. One weekend I went there to see Wabash run against Purdue University.

As I sat on the wall, my coach came over and asked whether I would help out. "The anchorman on the relay team just turned his ankle," he said. "Do you want to run it?"

Even though I wasn't yet fifteen years old and would be running against guys eighteen years and older, I said, "Sure."

I had to run in my bare feet because I didn't have any shoes, and luckily I was wearing short pants. But none of that was even remotely on my mind as the guy from Wabash handed me the baton. I could have been wearing a three-piece suit at that point, and it wouldn't have mattered. My only thought was to run and to run fast — and I did.

When I took off, the guy from Purdue was five yards ahead of me. I caught him before the last turn then passed him on the outside and crossed the finish line five yards ahead of him. I was more excited than I had ever been in my entire life. I took my blue ribbon home and told my parents.

My father never believed me. I knew it was far-fetched too, but it happened, and that night, as I went to bed, I thought, "My God, I am on my way to the Olympics."

That didn't happen, but the surprises kept coming. As a high school junior, I was elected class president — and I didn't even run! Someone else put my name on the ballot, and I arrived at school the next morning and saw my name on the bulletin board: Class President: Dick Van Dyke. The next year someone put my name on the ballot again, and I lost by two votes to Chuck Linley, a guy who said I hadn't done a thing the previous year — and he was right! I was too busy socializing.

A few months later, in the middle of my senior year, I left high school to join the Air Force — another unexpected twist. And so it has gone.

I never had an agenda. I didn't know I was going to sing or dance. I went from radio to nightclubs to TV to singing and dancing onstage in *Bye Bye Birdie.* It was all about feeding my family, not developing a career. I nearly got canned from *Bye Bye*

Birdie; they considered letting me go as we workshopped it in Philadelphia. I had no idea.

In my audition I had confessed that I didn't know how to dance. Gower Champion, the show's director, had said, "We'll teach you." Still, I was a novice — and nervous.

A year and a half later I won the Tony Award as Best Featured Actor, which was not only a surprise but a total shock. Adding to that, by then I had left the play and was shooting *The Dick Van Dyke Show* in Los Angeles. Charles Nelson Reilly accepted the award for me, but he didn't call afterward, and the telegram notifying me got stuck under our front doormat. Our housekeeper found it three days later.

Mary Poppins is yet another example of life saying, "Surprise!" Walt Disney heard me say during an interview that I thought there was a paucity of children's entertainment. From that, I got the job. And look at the way things worked out. Believe me, when I think of all the things that happened raising four children — the grades and graduations, the phone calls from family and friends about engagements, babies, grandchildren, great-grandchildren, jobs, promotions, and so on — the list of surprises that comprise life, my life, has been constant.

And then came the latest: marriage. Eight months after getting engaged, on Leap Day 2012, Arlene and I drove up the canyon in the hills behind us to the Serra Retreat, a serene spot embodying the philosophy of its namesake, Blessed Junipero Serra: "Always go forward, never turn back." I couldn't have moved forward fast enough. As I told the retreat's longtime priest, Father Warren Rouse, I was in a hurry — I wanted to make sure Arlene didn't get away.

I wasn't joking either. Our prenup had taken longer than expected, then our marriage license expired and had to be renewed, and getting family and friends together was nearly as hard as convincing Arlene to say yes. In the end that extra twenty-ninth day in February proved useful, as we finally traded "I Dos" in front of a handful of family and friends. Arlene looked beautiful in a simple red dress, while I went for understated elegance in a black suit with a festive silver tie.

"This was one of the smartest moves I've ever made," I told everyone as we celebrated at our house with high tea sandwiches, scones, clotted cream, and red velvet cake.

In September we celebrated with family

and friends in a blowout at our friends Fay and Frank Mancuso's beachfront home. Arlene created what she called "a sea-foam circus theme" party: "It's Jules Verne meets Moulin Rouge meets Fellini," she told me. Under a giant tent the extravaganza featured a circus barker who changed accents and languages as the night went on, jugglers, fan dancers, a dancing bear, dancing jelly fish, special lighting effects, popcorn, cotton candy, a sea of cupcakes, a gorgeous mermaid playing a harp, and a contortionist who floated in a crystal ball in the swimming pool overlooking the Pacific Ocean.

There was also a stack of hula hoops that all the guests took a spin with. Even the catering staff gave them a whirl! One of the many highlights of the evening was watching Arlene's mother hula-hoop to the song "Walking on Sunshine" in its entirety. Arlene and I capped the evening with a duet of the *Annie Get Your Gun* tune "Old Fashioned Wedding." It was the best wedding I'd ever been to — and best of all, I was in it!

In the weeks and months afterward I was asked the same question, repeatedly, but in umpteen different ways. Sometimes it came at me from behind embarrassed grins; other times it followed nervous hemming and hawing. Sometimes it was asked directly. Other times I had to decipher the round-about-ness of curiosity cloaked in a maze of modesty. But all wanted to know the same thing: Was there was still romance at my age? I'm sure my response gave a lot of people hope, as I said, "There's a reason these years are called the golden years."

This is the biggest surprise of all, I suppose. Love is everything when you are thirteen. It is everything when you are in your twenties and thirties. Finding it again is everything if you lose it in your forties or fifties. You cherish it in your sixties and seventies. And it is just as powerful and intoxicating if you are lucky enough to have it in your eighties and nineties.

It is all about love.

Maybe that should not be a surprise.

LOVE IN THE AFTERNOON

For me, having lived for a long time, having been through relationships, I have gotten over the romantic notion about love. Oh, there is still plenty of romance — flowers, dancing, moonlight walks. What I'm talking about is the possessiveness, the jealousy, all the evil and vain things. Real love, as I have come to know it, is when you care about the other person as much as you care about yourself. You can't make another person happy, but you can pave the way for them to make themselves happy.

Old Dogs, New Tricks

Though I am ninety, my wife has a thing for an even older man — my dog. Make that *our* dog, Rocky. A brown wire hair terrier, he is fourteen years old, which in dog years is equivalent to ninety-eight. They love each other. He especially loves Arlene. If he senses she has strayed too far or has been away from him for too long, he barks, and barks, and barks, until she comes around and pats him on the head, gives him a kiss, or cradles him in her lap while rubbing his belly. "I'm here," she says, comforting him into submission, and quiet.

She would never tolerate such demanding behavior from me or anyone else. But he is different. At night, when we are in bed watching TV, they are a pair. He sits directly in front of her, staring up at her with Jean-Paul Belmondo eyes: dark, droopy, lovelorn puddles of sadness and sensuality, demanding attention, waiting to drown her with affection. Either that, or he is struggling to make her out through thick layers of cloudiness (not cataracts) that have rendered his vision a misty morning fog. He doesn't move until she returns his gaze and then purrs, "I love you, Rocky."

Theirs is another relationship that defies the odds. When I met Arlene, she was a cat person, and she still is. She brought her cat, Spider, into the house and kept him in a carrying crate to protect him from Rocky, who kept jumping at her out of curiosity. Michelle had been allergic to cats; Rocky had never seen one before. And Spider didn't seem too keen on having a dog pawing at her. He'd let out blood-curdling screeches and foam at the mouth. In other words, he was not interested. I was discouraged. I wanted them to get along.

"It's going to take time," Arlene counseled.

That's how it was with Arlene and Rocky. At the start of our relationship she said, "I don't really like dogs." It was matter of fact. A declaration. To me, that was like saying, "I don't like Mozart" or "I don't like ice cream sundaes." What kind of person doesn't like dogs? I found out. But I did not hold that against Arlene, and neither did Rocky, and fortunately Arlene did not hold being a dog person or being a dog against either of us.

I understood the problem. Rocky was demanding. The first time Arlene came over to fix dinner, he dropped his plastic toy at her feet and waited for her to pick it up. She didn't. The next time she came over he put his toy at her feet and waited. After a bit she kicked the toy about three feet. He hurried over, scooped it up in his mouth, and deposited it back at her feet. When she failed to kick it again, he trained his Belmondos on her, but without the desired effect.

Over time she generously tossed the toy a few times. Rocky was grateful for the attention, I'm sure. But he was like an alcoholic with that toy. One toss was too many and a thousand was never enough. When Arlene began living at the house, she stayed in Michelle's room, and late at night, as she was drifting off, nestled in that comfortable world between being awake and asleep, she heard the door creak open.

She peered through the darkness, unable to see or hear anything — until suddenly a twenty-five-pound wire hair terrier jumped up on the bed and curled up on her pillow. "Get up, you dog!" she said, only to be met by a woozy grunt and a repositioned paw —

body language that said, "I ain't moving."

Not long after that fateful night, Arlene came out for breakfast one morning — followed closely by Rocky — and said, "Okay, we have a dog now." She quickly added, "But I'm still a cat person."

Though her cat Spider was wary of this new relationship, I was delighted. Rocky, well, he was in love. He wouldn't leave Arlene alone. He followed her everywhere. One afternoon Arlene picked up the leash. Rocky was right behind her. I was at the dining room table and overheard her talking to him.

"I love cats," Arlene said. "But the thing I don't like about cats is you can't take them for a walk. So, yeah, Rocky, I'll take you for a walk."

Thirty minutes later the front door opened. They were back — and Arlene was smiling.

"How was it?" I asked.

"Fun," she said. "We had a good walk."

Soon Arlene acknowledged she'd become a dog person. But she was not the only one who had changed. Rocky and I were living different lives, too. Aside from being married and upbeat again, I was ushered (or dragged) into the twenty-first century. I was on Twitter. I starred in six-second videos called Vines. I listened to music with Pandora, whose algorithms were like magic to me. I had no idea how that app did what it did (true confession: I don't even know what an app is), nor did I understand why, when I created the Tomaso Albinoni station, they never played any of the Italian Baroque composer's music. Nevertheless, I played it for hours.

Through Arlene I found new music from Lady Gaga, who sings great, and Amy Winehouse, who impressed me as part Billie Holiday, part Ella Fitzgerald, but with a sound of her own. She had clearly done her homework. The impact all of this had on me — from going to belly dancing class with Arlene to discovering new music to using apps — was an elixir all its own. I sang and danced constantly. It was like the wind suddenly picked up after being becalmed for a period of time.

I was moving again, invested in the future, growing, learning, and doing all the things that should not stop just because you get to a certain stage in life, or a ripe old age. Old age shouldn't be considered ripe; neither should it be thought of as overripe. It takes nine months to have a baby. People go to school for twelve to twenty-five years. Becoming educated takes even longer. And learning is — or should be — a process that spans an entire lifetime.

I was reminded of this recently when I read that Stewart Stern had died. Stewart was the Oscar-nominated screenwriter of *Rebel Without a Cause, The Ugly American, Teresa, Sybil,* and many other movies. But this man, who lived to be ninety-two, impressed me most with the way he lived his life.

I met him in the 1960s through Edna McHugh, one of Eddie Cantor's five daughters, and composer Jimmy McHugh's daughter-in-law. She was one of those sophisticated characters who knew everyone, and she hosted fabulous dinner parties where she gathered the most fascinating mix of writers, actors, artists, and musicians. The dinners I attended at her house inevitably ended with some kind of intellectual brain game. There was no sitting around chatting; after dessert it was a competition of cleverness and wit.

Stewart was among the brightest and most entertaining people there. He loved animals, and I remember him telling a story about how, while on a hike, he came upon a pasture of grazing cows and laid down in the grass among the animals. Another time he related being on a safari in Africa, wandering into the jungle, and camping solo among the wildlife. He was a gentle, quiet man who gave me the sense that his writing was about his own personal search for something other than show business, perhaps something purer and closer to his soul.

Indeed, he ended up a beloved writing teacher in Seattle after moving from Hollywood in the late 1980s, according to his obituary, in order to "get away from all the outside voices and pressures, and back to what inspired me to write in the first place." I was about that same age, my middle sixties, and in Denver, working on the first season of *Diagnosis Murder,* when I heard about this thing called Toaster from Amiga that let you create animations on your computer. I was a life-long cartoonist — or amateur doodler. I drew caricatures of people when I was on the set. So I couldn't resist this new toy.

I ordered one. It came to the hotel, and I plugged it in. I read the instruction book. I had a camera. I took a picture of the skyline, and ten minutes later I had spaceships flying over Denver. I was hooked. I described it to coworkers as a combination of technology and art, but in truth it was playtime. Of course, in those days, if you finished a small, fifteen-frame animation on Friday, it took until Monday to render. Now it's very fast. But time didn't matter to me.

This was a hobby, and like any hobbyist, I was more than willing to fritter away hours, if not days, pursuing a project. I ended up doing quite a bit of CG animation for the series, including a fiery motorcycle crash that opened one episode. The show didn't have a budget for big stunts like that, so I shot a highway scene, went back to my computer, added a motorcycle, and created the crash, all in CG. We used it, and I got paid $200. I still create animations at the computer in my studio. The process is bottomless, and inevitably, as I whittle away the hours, I discover something new.

But I was telling you about Arlene and Rocky. Let me get back to them because the point I want to emphasize here is that old dogs can, should, and need to learn new tricks. It's the reason Rocky is still with us — that, and my wife's devotion to him. Their first walk together led to daily romps in the meadow on the hill. Arlene would return home eager to describe the way Rocky bounded through the tall grass, an old man running like a spirited pup happy to be out in the fresh air.

Then his eyes got worse and hips weakened. The decline was gradual until late

2014. He struggled to get up and wobbled on his legs. It seemed like he had back pain. Arlene took him to vet, who delivered a grave prognosis: "You're going to have to put him down. It's pretty much over." Arlene came home in tears.

I pictured Rocky as a pup, scampering near the pool. He had lived a wonderful life, I thought, and I was ready to surrender to the doctor's end-of-life prognosis, if that was most humane. But Arlene made it clear that *her dog* was not going anyplace. She wasn't going to allow anyone to put him down just because he had developed a disability, just because he had gotten old.

"Except for his legs, everything else is working," she said. She picked him up. Momentarily tense, he looked at her through opaque blue eyes, then relaxed, like a pup, and licked her face. "See that," she said.

"He loves his mom," I said.

Arlene smiled. "We wouldn't put a human being down just because they have trouble getting around."

My brother disagreed. Jerry thought Rocky should be put down. "He's old," he said without seeing the similarities between him and Rocky. Both of them were old. Both of them had bad hips, bad backs, and various other aches and pains that kept them from getting around the way they did in their youth. Both of them sat around much of the day. Both of them barked if the women in their lives weren't by their side, albeit affectionately, but essentially demanding the same thing: "Come pay attention to me."

As I have mentioned, Rocky barked nonstop when he started to miss Arlene. Jerry had zero tolerance for the noise, especially when he was exercising in the pool. "That dog should be put down!" he kept telling her.

Arlene frowned as she scooped up Rocky and wrapped her arms protectively around him while the dog's appreciative tongue searched for her cheek. "Come on, Jerry," she said sweetly. "We don't say such things about you!"

This version of The Sunshine Boys played daily in the backyard. Then one afternoon, as Arlene was walking Rocky by the pool, the dog's hip wobbled. He lost his balance and fell into the pool.

"Oh no!" Arlene gasped, before taking a breath and preparing to jump in to rescue Rocky. A moment later, though, she was still on the side, frozen with disbelief by what she was saw. Rocky was swimming. As soon as he hit the water, his back legs started to work, effortlessly, the way they were supposed to but couldn't on land. But in the water they did not have to bear any weight. The salt water added even more buoyancy. As Arlene later recalled to me, he almost appeared to be smiling. He was suddenly Rocky Phelps.

One dip in the pool, of course, did not make Rocky a young pup again. But after that he went swimming every day. Spider would sit on a chaise, watching supportively. We thought she knew his eyesight had gone, and she felt more secure; she also wanted Arlene's attention. As for Rocky, we could tell he anticipated his daily swim with a puppy-like eagerness. Once in the water, his tail wagged with such velocity it looked like a propeller.

Actually, his workout was more like therapy — and similar to the routine of . . . guess who? In fact, pretty soon my brother and Rocky were alternating time in the pool. They were taking the same pain pills and doing the same water therapy for the same amount of time. It was as if they had received a prescription for what I always preach — keep moving!

And it helped. The old dogs had new tricks, and they were better off for it.

Did I mention that I also fell in love with Spider? I'm now a dog *and* a cat person.

Old dogs. New tricks.

That should be on a T-shirt or a bumper sticker.

Look, people don't want to deal with dogs that get old and are no longer perfect, and the same is true when human beings incur the wear and tear of a long life. Despite the old adage, though, old dogs *can* learn new tricks — and should! I have seen the benefits in my own backyard. We don't know how long Rocky will be with us, but right now he is doing well. Some days, thanks to Arlene, he gets more exercise than I do. He seems to smile when she lifts his hind legs and walks him around the backyard like a wheelbarrow. He has his own wheelchair. The vet says he seems content and happy. His tail wags throughout the day. He has added acupuncture, laser therapy, and a workout on a water treadmill to his weekly routine, and from what I can see, he continues to enjoy being a dog.

My brother is trudging along too. Life may slow down, but it shouldn't stop. Every day you wake up and don't find yourself listed in the obituary is an opportunity to take charge of your health — and your happiness.

Old dogs. New tricks.
Live the life. Get the T-shirt.

WHY WRITE IT DOWN?

I keep a notebook by my bed
and lay out the day that's ahead.
When it's there on the page,
my thoughts disengage,
and my brain turns to dreaming instead.

Other Tips and Truths About Old Age

TRUTH: They say the knees are the second thing to go. They're wrong.

TRUTH: Money can't buy happiness. But it can pay for good doctors and medicine.

TIP: If a doctor tells you he can make you look twenty years younger, don't believe him. Everybody will notice. And nobody will think you look twenty years younger.

TIP: Collect experiences, not memories.

TRUTH: You are never too old for romance. A candlelight dinner, a slow dance, a stroll under the stars — these are as potent and magical at eighty-five as they were at twenty-five.

TRUTH: After a hundred, everything should be free. It's not — but it should be.

TIP: Health foods no longer matter after eighty years old. At that point eat anything you want for the rest of your life. That's healthy!

TIP: Look your age. But don't act it.

TRUTH: Most people aren't as grown-up as they look.

TRUTH: Some of life is planning. A lot of it is luck.

TIP: Forgiveness is the best sleeping pill.

TIP: Old age is not the time to be scared. Instead, be curious.

TRUTH: Yes, you wasted too much time worrying about things that didn't matter.

TRUTH: When you answer every question by asking, "What?" it means you are hard of hearing, not old.

TIP: If your children tell you that you are wearing your pants too high or your sweater is inside out, they are probably right.

TIP: It doesn't matter if you can no longer remember your grandchildren's birthdays anymore. Or even your children's birthdays. They'll remind you.

TRUTH: As you get older, you start to shrink. But your heart still retains the capacity to grow and expand.

TRUTH: A spoonful of sugar really does help the medicine go down.

TIP: New experiences are the only things you can collect in life that end up being worth it.

TIP: Carry a tiny flashlight with you. It's helpful in dark restaurants.

TRUTH: All the different ways you thought you might die by now didn't happen. That's a good thing!

TRUTH: Social Security is the only security you have in life. Let's hope that doesn't get screwed up.

TIP: Easy Street doesn't exist. Stop looking for it or wishing you had found it.

TRUTH: Parties were more fun before everyone else was dead. But don't let that ruin your time.

TRUTH: Old people really do know most of the answers to life's important questions. But no one knows if there really is a God.

TIP: Don't take it all so seriously.

TIP: Everything really does looks better in the morning.

TRUTH: In the end you realize only two things matter — love and hope — and as you get closer to the end, it's only love.

TRUTH: Life goes on.

Good Health Without Drugs . . . Sort Of

About ten years ago I was in New York when I was beset by a mystery affliction. It was afternoon, and I returned to my hotel to take a nap. I got comfortable on the bed, and moments later it started. My brain felt like it was expanding and contracting, pushing against the inside of my skull. It didn't hurt. It was simply weird and something I knew wasn't normal.

My nap never happened, and for the next few months the same odd sensation of my brain expanding and contracting interrupted future attempts at afternoon sleeps. Then it started to wake me up in the morning. It was not anything sharp or unbearable — nothing that made me wince or scream or run for the medicine chest in search of a quick fix. I did think the T-word, tumor, but only briefly. I didn't dwell on it.

Maybe it's my easygoing constitution, but I felt it more as a distraction. After it woke me up, I rubbed my temples and squeezed the sides of my head, trying to massage whatever it was away. Eventually it would go away — for a little bit. Then it would return.

Each time was a sneak attack. There was no warning or predictability. As I told my doctor, there was a sort of regular irregularity to its onset. If I anticipated the feeling, it didn't happen. If I forgot about it, the knocking arrived, like an eye twitch or a muscle spasm. This went on for months, and then months turned into years.

I saw specialists, who sent me to different specialists. I was given brain scans, CAT scans, a spinal tap, and numerous other tests. I called the Mayo Clinic, hoping to schedule an examination there, but they said I had already had every test. I went back to my doctor. He was stymied.

"About the only thing we know for sure is it's not fatal," he said. "You've done all the tests."

"So you don't know . . ." My voice trailed off. I hoped he would finish my sentence.

"It's a mystery," he said, closing my folder and, presumably, my case. "I'm sorry. I wish we knew. I wish I could tell you there was something you could take. A magic pill. But there's nothing I can give you."

Nothing he could give me? It had to be the only malady on record (even if it was only my record) for which medical science had not invented a pill. I had never heard of an ailment for which there was not a medicine. It is almost un-American. According to research I found online, seven out of ten people in this country take a prescription drug, and more than half take two. The most popular medications include antibiotics, painkillers, and antidepressants, and not far behind are pills for high blood pressure and cholesterol.

I am not taking any of those, something for which I thank my parents for every day. Good genes — I have been lucky that way. I have enjoyed good health without drugs . . . sort of. In the 1960s, back when I was holding down jobs in both TV and theater, I started taking sleeping pills, as many Americans did, and I still take one nearly every night. A good night's sleep is habit-forming, I suppose. I also take Vicodin when my arthritis acts up. Otherwise, having quit alcohol and cigarettes decades ago, I am practically as pure as filtered water.

But still, I am not anti-prescription medication. I am also pro-over-the-counter medicine if it helps. Imagine the scratching, sniffling, and swelling in a world without

Benadryl. Drugs are the Band-Aids that keep many of us here. And with the majority of Americans on them, they are also potentially great conversation starters.

According to the statistics, you can go up to almost anyone and ask, "What are you taking? How's that working for you?" Total strangers have something in common to talk about, especially those who have acquired a lot of chronology: "Do you get generic? What's your co-pay? Where do you go to get it filled — Walgreen's? CVS? How's the line there?" Those are not bad questions.

As the miles pile up, you realize how much we all have in common: baseball, barbeques, hamburgers, homework, jobs, the desire for companionship, children, TV shows, . . . allergy pills. As we get older, our similarities are more pronounced: gray hair, old clothes come back into style, grandchildren, good-byes, . . . restaurants close. When you get to be my age, now all that matters is family and health. Priorities become clear. Are you loved? Do you have someone to love back? And does anything hurt?

As all that related to me, well, nothing hurt per se, but I did have this persistent weirdness, that dull ache, in my head. I felt it early in the morning and when I tried to take a nap in the afternoon. Always without warning. As the years passed, I tried to park it in the back corner of things that mattered. It was my inconvenient reminder that life, if nothing else, is a mystery, that not everything can be figured out or cleared up with a prescription.

Then one day I made an appointment with a neuropsychiatrist friend, Dr. Hamlin Emory. Though it followed an episode, I scheduled the appointment more from a desire to figure out the mystery than the frustration with not having a remedy. Dr. Emory, a former Malibu neighbor who practiced in West Los Angeles, was a brilliant man, a bracing intellectual, and an unabashed contrarian, particularly when it came to practicing medicine — and with the way medicine is practiced.

As he explained in our initial consultation, he didn't treat symptoms. Instead he approached symptoms as indicators that the brain was out of balance. His thesis was based on research that the brain's main job was to keep the body running and that the majority of its work went into regulating the myriad autonomic systems that keep us alive. A symptom like the weirdness in my head was a sign that something was out of kilter.

"Physiology generates mentality," he said,

breaking his thesis down to its most basic components. "Mentality does not generate physiology. You may be able to train yourself to a certain degree to alter your physiology somewhat, but in terms of your visceral brain, you're not going to alter those genetic influences. And that's what I look at when I examine you."

He gave me a thorough diagnostic workup, covering the gamut — physical, mental, psychological, and biological, starting with an eight-page questionnaire that covered my family's medical history as far back as I knew it, along with my own history. His exam also included blood work and an assessment of my cognitive ability. He ordered brain scans. He also gave me an EEG, hooking electrodes up to my head to measure my brainwaves — the alpha and the delta, I think they are called — while explaining that the results would be the foundation of his diagnosis and any accompanying treatment.

In the most simplistic terms, he gathered a ton of information about what was wrong, what had been wrong in the past, and then he looked at the brain in a resting state, like a car idling, for insight into whatever was causing the misfire.

"I'm looking for the slightest irregularity

in the patterns," he explained as he went through the readouts.

Eventually he tapped his finger on the test results. It was his ah-ha revelation. He hypothesized that the relationship within my hypothalamic-pituitary-adrenal axis was slightly out of sync. It was not spiking as high as it should, he said, and that could be the reason for the pulsing sensations that had bothered me and baffled other doctors for years.

"Think of the hypothalamus as the orchestra conductor," Dr. Emory said. "He tells the musicians to play faster or slower, or louder or softer. It's like Zubin Mehta, the longtime conductor of the Los Angeles Philharmonic, used to do — except the members aren't able to play like they did before. In my opinion, that's happening in this part of your brain. The conductor of your orchestra is getting a performance that's a little less vehement than it should be, resulting in a homeostatic failing that is very likely the palpitation you experience."

"I think we need to focus on increasing the dopaminergic activity," he continued, "and by doing that, improve the brain's neurophysiology, adjusting your awake cycle — or your diurnal or quotidian rhythm — so that it improves to where you can take a nap or have a decent night's sleep without being interrupted by the palpitations."

Dr. Emory prescribed a drug called Nuvigil, a mood enhancer that would provide an "up-regulation in amplitude," as he put it. The drug had been developed to keep military pilots awake and alert over long periods of time. Air traffic controllers used it too. He thought the increase in amplitude might decrease the lows, return balance, and let me rest without the palpitations. At the same time, he warned that drugs don't work on everyone, and he didn't know whether Nuvigil would work for me.

"If there are adverse effects, they don't fit," he said. "The trick is to find the drug that fits you."

I began taking one pill every so often — for instance, before performances or interviews — and found it sharpened my thinking and elevated my mood slightly. It took me from a seven to a nine, making me feel the way I did thirty years earlier: sharp, quick, and bright. I thought everyone should try it. But when I gave one to my brother, he went bananas. It caused my friend Bob Palmer's heart rate to spike — he hated it. Arlene couldn't sleep or catch her breath for three days after she tried one. I quit experimenting on my family and friends.

As good as it made me feel, Nuvigil didn't stop the weird feeling of my brain expanding and contracting. But it did diminish the frequency of the palpitations, as Dr. Emory had suggested it might, enabling me to take more naps and sleep longer most mornings. And that was okay with me.

Ten years into this thing, I know that one pill doesn't necessarily lead to a cure for anything. But I'm fine with a compromise, especially one that lets me keep moving. I do not wait and wonder whether the sensation that started all of this will manifest itself today, tomorrow, next month, or ever again. At this point I know it is not terminal. Terminal is bad. Annoying is something I can deal with. I don't dwell on the negative. That's crucial to keep in mind as the machinery slows and wears out. Perspective is as important as any pill — even more important, as I think about it.

The best medicine comes from within. Even my friend Dr. Emory, who asserts that mentality doesn't influence physiology, agrees with me when it comes to ignoring the onset of old age. I asked him, "If sixty is the new forty, as I heard on one of the morning news shows, and eighty is the new sixty, what is the key to feeling and acting young?"

He pointed at me. "Genetics is number one," he says. "You hope and pray for the kind of genetic endowment you were bequeathed. Beyond that, be the person who finds the diamond in the haystack. Have a good attitude. Be able to entertain yourself. I think the essential ingredient to being joyful in life is to have stuff you enjoy doing and then to do it. Let me ask you something."

"Sure."

"Do you dance like you did twenty-five years ago?"

"No."

"But you haven't stopped."

"No, I haven't."

"Right. You've continued to refine yourself as you move through time. Though people deal with a range of issues that come with age, I think the concern has to be less on what is lost and more on continuing to evolve, learn, grow, change, and develop new talents. It's the difference between being a spectator and a participant. Too many people become spectators instead of continuing to initiate new chapters in their own adventure. But you get the most joy from doing what you are passionate about in the world. You have to keep doing it.

"Chronology eventually gets the best of

all of us in that we experience to some degree a reversal of physical prowess. So you ask, then what? Well, I point to children who are not unlike older people at this stage. Both have limited physical prowess. Both can be dependent on others for care. However, a child of three, four, and five still has fun. Even as your capacities may limit you, you can still have fun. You can still play in your mind. In fact, this kind of self-amusement is essential."

Very true.

But how ironic that this whole thing started ten years ago when, like a child, I wanted to take a nap — which I may do right now.

NINETY YEARS — A REPORT CARD

For some reason people think I am a conservative. This has been the case for many years. I don't know what I have said or done to create that impression. But when I walk into a restaurant, a shopping mall, or an airport terminal, the same thing happens. A certain type of person makes a beeline to me, apologizes for interrupting, and then launches into a monologue: "Here's what we need to do about the immigration problem!" Or, "The gays — what are we going to do about them, Dick?" Or, "Remember when this country was great?"

As a matter of fact, I do remember what this country was like over the past ninety years. I have witnessed more events, changes, and innovations than most of the 300 million people situated between Malibu and Maine. There used to be an attraction at Disneyland called Walt Disney's Carousel of Progress that showed the technological advances in homes through the decades as the world modernized. I have experienced that in real life.

When I was born, Calvin Coolidge was the president of the United States, the dust from World War I was still settling, construction on the Empire State building was just beginning, John Dillinger and Bonnie and Clyde were kind of public heroes — celebrities of the day, if you will — and the entire population of Danville, Illinois, where I grew up, used to run outside and look skyward on those rare occasions when an airplane flew overhead. In other words, I have seen a lot of changes in my time.

Here's my take on some of the headline-making people and events that have mattered to me from 1925 to the present (keep in mind that the grades are my opinion — but hey, it's my book):

1925

Tennessee schoolteacher John T. Scopes, who was born in Kentucky but coincidentally raised in my hometown of Danville, was arrested for violating state law against teaching the theory of evolution in class. This was but an initial chapter of a long-running debate that continues to pit fundamentalists against science. The reason behind his arrest: **A**

The country's malingering failure to separate fact from fiction in the classroom ninety years later: **F**

The 1960 movie loosely based on the Scopes trial, *Inherit the Wind,* starring Spencer Tracy: **A**

The Great Gatsby by F. Scott Fitzgerald was published. I tried reading it once when I was younger. I made it halfway through, but I enjoyed it: **A**

Mein Kampf by Adolf Hitler was published. Never read it. Don't plan to. The world could have done without it: **F**

Al Capone took over the Chicago bootlegging racket. Combining ambition and bullets, he kept Americans liquored up during the Prohibition Era and laid the groundwork for numerous books and movies: **F**

1927

Philo Farnsworth invented the television, and thank goodness he did. In the 1940s and 1950s it enabled me to feed my family. Then with *The Dick Van Dyke Show,* it changed my life in every way imaginable — and some you can't imagine. Like the first time I realized people recognized me.

It was soon after the show began airing and I was driving my family to Las Vegas. We stopped in Barstow for breakfast, and on the way out of the restaurant a group of teenage girls ran toward us, screaming, "It's him. He's on TV." It scared the hell out of us. We got in the car and plowed out of there.

But being on TV was the greatest thing that ever happened to me. In general it has defined our lives and given humanity shared experiences. We've cried together, we've gasped together, and we have laughed together. My taste and sensibilities are rooted in a different era, but I appreciate the choices we have now, and I'm in awe at the way we can summon shows from the cloud and stream them on computers, tablets, and phones: **A**

1930

My parents took me to see Al Jolson in *The Jazz Singer,* the first real "talkie." I was hooked: **A**

1932

Franklin D. Roosevelt was elected the thirty-second president of the United States. I remember the election results broadcast on the radio and the jubilation that followed his victory. The country was in the thick of the Great Depression. They needed a leader, someone to believe in, and FDR was the man. The big song was "Happy Days Are Here Again," and you heard it everywhere, playing on the radio: **A**

1933

FDR got rid of the Volstead Act right away and launched the New Deal. My father hated him. He would yell at the radio, "People, go out and get a job! Don't live off the government!" I loved Roosevelt. Even at eight years old, I thought he was a good orator. He had gravitas. He was solid. As I listened to him, I would say to myself, "This is a good president." And as time went on, I thought he got better. I lived across the street from a public park where I took music lessons, participated in shows, got on a sports team, and did art — everything was free. It was all WPA sponsored, and I took advantage of it. I didn't understand why my father and other Republicans hated him so much. I thought FDR was saving the country's ass: **A**

The Marx Brothers released *Duck Soup,* and Laurel and Hardy released *Sons of the Desert.* The Marx Brothers' jokes were a little over my head — I didn't quite get them, except for the physical part. I loved Laurel and Hardy. From the get-go Stan Laurel was my comic idol: **A+**

1934
John Dillinger was killed. I remember hearing news reports about Bonnie and Clyde, Baby Face Nelson, and Pretty Boy Floyd, but Dillinger was the most notorious of all these bank robbers. I was listening to the radio when I heard that the FBI had shot him in a Chicago movie theater. I thought, *Wow, they got him.* Dillinger: **D**

FBI Agent Melvin Purvis: **A**

1935
The Benny Goodman Jazz Orchestra plays on the *Let's Dance* radio program for the first time. I don't remember that specific broadcast, probably because it came on late at night, but I do remember my dad introducing me to swing. I was hooked immediately. I loved music. I was always an

enthusiastic singer, whether at home, in the church choir, or in the school chorus. In sixth grade my voice changed to a bass, and I had to sing with the eighth-grade music class.

In junior high I was the first trombone in the school band. I was taller than anyone, so they figured I had the reach. I was given the first seat only because my good buddy, Al Hoss, who sat in the second chair, didn't read music as quickly as me. But I envied his tone. My downfall as a player was the state band championship. We got to the state finals, where our number featured a trombone solo. I had practiced it numerous times and had the piece down. But when it counted, I stepped forward, looked out at the audience, which seemed like thousands of people to me, and froze. It was pure stage fright. I didn't play a note. The conductor looked like he wanted to kill me. I never played another note on the trombone again.

I played the piano instead. We had an old upright at home, and from the time I was a little kid, I would sit on the bench and figure out how to read the music. One day after choir practice at church, the organist heard me fooling around on the church piano. I was playing "Claire de Lune" before it changes keys.

He said, "You have talent. I'll give you free piano lessons." I only went twice, one of the mistakes of my life because I would love to play with proper technique today. But I still played all the time. In high school my buddy and I played four-handed boogie woogie. We were the boogie woogie kings of our school. So Benny Goodman, swing, and jazz: **A+**

This was also the year my grandfather died. He went into the hospital one day for a tonsillectomy, suffered a burst aneurysm, and dropped dead on the spot. He was only fifty-five years old and seemingly in perfect shape, if not still physically imposing from his job in the railroad's tool shop. I was busted up. I remember talking to my brother about it. Jerry was only five years old at the time, and I tried to explain death to him. He didn't understand that our grandfather was gone — it was too hard for him to grasp. I don't know that I came to terms with it either. I looked at the obituaries every day without finding his name. As far as I know, my grandfather was never listed. It bothered me. My grandfather: **A**

Death: **F**

The mid-1930s was the heyday of Jack Benny's radio show. Around this time he went from CBS to NBC, and the American public went with him. Television hadn't come along yet. On a summer evening you could sit outside, and all you would hear were porch swings creaking, crickets chirping, and Jack Benny coming from every house up and down the street. Jack Benny: A

1939

World War II broke out with Nazi Germany's invasion of Poland and France, and England declared war on Germany. At age fourteen, I remember thinking that it was about time. Fighting across Europe had been going on for a while, and then the big escalation: Hitler bombed London flat, and I was terribly bothered that the United States wasn't doing anything. As France fell to Germany and Italy, I remember wondering what we were waiting for. Were they waiting until Hitler got to the United States?

We listened to reports every night on the radio and watched newsreels at the movie theater. Our entry into the war seemed inevitable, though the wait for Washington to make a move seemed interminable — so much was at stake. The early years of World

1941

December 7: Japan attacked Pearl Harbor, "a date which will live in infamy." It was a Sunday, and some friends and I had gone to the movies that afternoon. As we walked out of the theater we sensed something was different even before we heard the news. It was that big. But everybody on the street was talking about it. Pearl Harbor had been bombed. I had never heard of Pearl Harbor before. No one knew we had a base in Hawaii. Then suddenly everybody knew. Pearl Harbor: **F**

1943

I joined the Air Force. Entering the military was something I never pictured for myself. I was still fifteen when the United States entered the war and thought it would be over before I reached draft age. Then in February, as the war dragged on and I looked ahead to my eighteenth birthday, I told my mother I was thinking of signing up before I came of draft age later that year.

In the biggest surprise of my life to that point, she said I was already eighteen. She explained that I had been born prematurely and that it was something not worth sharing. Well, my grandmother nearly spit out her coffee when she heard me recount that story. She told me the truth: I was born out of wedlock. Regardless, I hurried to the nearest Air Force recruiting center before I was drafted and sent to the front lines. Instead, I went into the special services, for entertainers. Avoiding the front lines: **A**

Me as a soldier: **C**

1945
The war ended. I was let out of the service because I was no longer of service. I remember hearing news that Hitler had killed himself. I was shocked and sickened by the reports and the pictures of the death camps where Nazi soldiers had murdered millions of Jews. It was incomprehensible. Nobody could believe that human beings could be so horrific in our modern times. War: **F**

Victory: **A**

Discharge from the service: **A**

In August the United States dropped atomic bombs on two Japanese cities, Hiroshima and Nagasaki. For some reason I don't remember where I was either of those times, but I do recall a heaviness of spirit, a feeling of dullness from the ensuing victory and thinking it was a sad time for the country. However, I admired President Truman for making a tough decision, and by God, when he ran again, I voted for him. He wasn't a great orator, but he spoke the simple truth — and he didn't lie. "If you can't stand the heat, get out of the kitchen." America's war effort: **A**

Truman's effort: **A**

My effort in war: **C** (I did my best, but it can't compare with those who fought.)

1947
I bought my first TV. I was in Los Angeles and came home with one of those early sets with the seven-inch screen. There wasn't much to watch, mostly news and serials. At night the networks shut down and put on a test pattern. But I was glued to it. It was radio with pictures, and I knew it was going to catch on.

1949
I happened to be in New York City during the original Broadway run of Arthur Miller's *Death of a Salesman*. It was a sensa-

tion out of the box, I recall, with wonderful reviews, and I went to see it the first chance I had. Gene Lockhart had taken over the role of Willy Loman from Lee J. Cobb, and he was a force on that stage — too much for me. Willy Loman was my father, a traveling salesman. It was so close to my own childhood. I was depressed for a month. **A**

1952

Singing in the Rain, starring Gene Kelly, Donald O'Connor, and Debbie Reynolds, was released. I was working at the Million Dollar Theatre in downtown Los Angeles doing five-a-day vaudeville shows with my partner, Phil Erickson. We called ourselves the Merry Mutes. I must have seen *Singing in the Rain* twenty times, and it never got old. I think it's the best movie musical ever made. **A**

1956

Elvis Presley hit it big. I never understood him. I was not a fan of the music. In fact, before Elvis took rock 'n' roll to a new popularity, Bill Haley had his own early rock 'n' roll hits with "Rock Around the Clock" and "Shake, Rattle and Roll," and I felt the same way about his music. Years later I was in a coffee shop, and he came up to my table and introduced himself. He was a nice man. I jokingly said, "I don't know whether to shake your hand or punch you." Those songs weren't music to me. As far as I was concerned, they ruined everything. **D**

1957
I saw Mike Nichols and Elaine May perform at Town Hall in New York City, and to this day it remains the most brilliant comedy performance I have seen onstage. In what I remember as the final sketch, they started out as two kids playing house. As it progressed and they grew up and became adults, their dialogue got harsher, until Nichols and May were in a fight. Stagehands came out and separated them. Those of us in the audience thought, "Oh my God, they lost it." Then suddenly they turned and bowed. It was brilliant. **A**

1960
Nixon and Kennedy ran against each other in the presidential election. I had voted for Ike, Dwight D. Eisenhower, and I thought he did a good job. But I didn't consider myself a Republican. I watched the Nixon-Kennedy debate on television. I thought Kennedy won hands down. I was surprised when a number of people I knew who had

213

listened to the debate on the radio thought the opposite, that Nixon had been the clear winner. I was a fan of Kennedy. I was taken in by the Camelot Era; it was both smart and glamorous or glamorous and smart. I thought he was a good president. **A**

1961

The Dick Van Dyke Show premiered. I got a week off from *Bye Bye Birdie* to do the pilot. I was such a nervous wreck that I had four fever blisters. But the writing made it a cakewalk! The pilot went unbelievably well. The show wasn't a hit right away. We were up against the *Perry Como Show,* and my name didn't mean anything. We got canceled at the end of the season. But summer reruns helped, and Sheldon went to Proctor and Gamble and convinced them to stick with it. He said the show was too good to cancel. He was right.

We took off in season two, and though we only did five seasons, thanks to syndication the show has rarely been off the air. Why has it held up? Carl had a rule: No references to current events, no slang, nothing that would date it.

It also had to be real.

He would tell the writers, "I don't care how ridiculous a situation is as long as it

could really happen. It has to be believable."
And, of course, above all else, the shows
were funny. **A**

1963
President Kennedy was assassinated. I was
doing *The Dick Van Dyke Show*. I was at
work that day, November 22. I walked in
from lunch and saw the assistant director,
John Chulay, standing in front of the television, with tears streaming down his face.
He turned and said, "Kennedy was shot." I
had to record an album that night, *Songs I
Like, by Dick Van Dyke*. We'd already rented
the studio; the musicians in the orchestra
cried the entire night. It was so tragic. **F**

1963–1964
Color TV became the new standard. Although a handful of shows were broadcast
in color in the fifties, color TV was not
widely available until the early sixties. The
network approached Carl Reiner about doing *The Dick Van Dyke Show* in color, but
we stayed in black and white. Around this
same time I bought my family's first color
TV, an RCA. But I began seeing movies that
shouldn't have been in color, such as *Citizen
Kane* and *The Magnificent Ambersons*. It
took a while before the industry appreciated

that those were so beautiful in black and white. **A**

1964

With four children, including two girls, Beatlemania hit hard in our house. I am pretty sure the Beatles' Sunday night appearance on the *Ed Sullivan Show* was must-see TV for all of us, including me. Unlike Elvis and Bill Haley, I was impressed by the group's musicality. They were more sophisticated than anyone else. The next month my daughters, Carrie Beth and Stacy, were with me in England, where I was working on *Mary Poppins,* and we crossed paths with the Fab Four at Twickenham Studios.

We were working on the "Jolly Holiday" number, and John, Paul, George, and Ringo were finishing *A Hard Day's Night.* They invited all of us to a party, and we had a great time. But here's the best part: months later we were at a fundraiser somewhere, a garden party, and they came up to my daughters and said, "Hi, Stacy. Hi, Carrie. How are you?"

My daughters were blown away that the Beatles remembered their names. They probably still haven't gotten over it. The guys were nice young men, and I thought their music was very good. **A**

Mary Poppins was released. I knew this was a special project the day Walt Disney first showed me all the scenes beautifully painted as storyboards. They were tacked to the wall. It was like being in an art gallery. Then I sat and listened to the Sherman brothers play the score. That cinched it. I knew I had to be in that movie. Looking back, the magic was the music and Walt's touch. He just had it. There was a great spirit the whole time we made it, and I think it shows onscreen. **A+**

1965

On March 25 Dr. Martin Luther King Jr. led thousands of civil rights demonstrators on a march across the Edmund Pettus Bridge in Selma, Alabama. This followed a terrible display a few weeks earlier when police beat marchers as they attempted to peacefully cross the bridge on their way to the state capitol. The violence had been televised. Americans had seen peaceful citizens bloodied by police. That the demonstrators were black and the police white made it even uglier.

In the interim Dr. King urged religious leaders of all faiths to join his march. I wanted to go. A year earlier I had attended a rally at the Los Angeles Memorial Coliseum where Dr. King spoke. I had lived in Atlanta as a younger man and had seen — and in fact been shocked and disturbed by — the way black people were treated. I thought it was important to go to Selma. But *The Dick Van Dyke Show* was in production, and the studio wouldn't shut it down. But I give Dr. King and the Civil Rights Movement an **A.**

1969
Neil Armstrong walked on the moon. I was glued to the TV the whole time. In addition to the image of Armstrong climbing out of the lunar module, the other thing I can still picture is CBS anchor Walter Cronkite counting down the touchdown and then finally taking off his glasses and shaking his head in amazement. He was wiped out, as we all were, though I also remember thinking that the whole thing was a fake. Some people believed that it was all acted out in a soundstage. It reminded me of when I was a kid and the disappointment I felt when I learned there were no aliens on the moon. **A**

1971
The New Dick Van Dyke Show premiered. I reunited with Carl Reiner on this new CBS

sitcom, which costarred Hope Lange as my wife. It was a solid show, but it never took off because viewers wouldn't accept me with another woman. One day a lady came up to me in the supermarket, hit me with her purse, and said, "How could you leave that wonderful Laura?" I learned a lesson: thou shall not cheat — even on your TV wife. **B**

1972

Watergate consumed the country in so many ways. Among the most serious and long-lasting harm — at least to me — was the sense of mistrust the incident seemed to ignite in all aspects of American life. It was a wake-up call: What do you mean we can't trust the president? What do you mean he ordered a break-in? In 1974, two years after the break-in was uncovered, Nixon resigned. We are still paying a price. **F**

1975

With the fall of Saigon, the Vietnam War finally ended, and it was many years too late, as far as I was concerned. I was against the war from the beginning. I thought it was based on paranoia. Just like the Korean conflict, we didn't manage to do anything in Vietnam except lose a lot of lives. We got out by the skin of our teeth, as evidenced by those indelible images of Americans being hastily evacuated from rooftops as the North Vietnamese took over the southern capital. **F**

1980

Ronald Reagan was elected president of the United States. I thought back to when I first met him in the early 1960s. Actor Don De-Fore was a neighbor of mine, and he invited my wife, Margie, and me to a dinner party. It was Ozzie and Harriet Nelson, Ron and Nancy, and my wife and I. We were the only liberals at the table. But I kept my mouth shut. Ron talked that night about getting rid of the unions and the right-to-work issue. A short time later he served two terms as California's governor. Five years later he ran for president of the United States and was elected twice to what was, without question, his greatest role. Even though we differed politically, as a fellow actor, I will respectfully give him top marks: **A**

1984

The Summer Olympics were in Los Angeles, and I went for the whole thing. As a former track guy (I was a high jumper and ran the 220 in high school; I never had the stamina for the 440), I loved it. The city came together; it was a two-week celebration and showed the potential for people from all over to get along. **A**

1990

In February Nelson Mandela was released from jail after being in prison for thirty years. Four years later he was elected president of South Africa, the first black president in that country's history. Apartheid ended, and it seemed like a victory for the entire world. But I remember seeing Mandela on the news around then and noticing the look in his eyes. It was full of character and strength and, impressively, a depth of humanity that I had seen before — in Dr. Martin Luther King Jr. It was the kind of look that gave me faith that right does eventually triumph. **A**

1993

Diagnosis Murder premiered. As I mentioned earlier, producer Fred Silverman wanted me to star in a spinoff from *Jake and the Fatman.* "Freddy, I'm ninety-five years old. I can't do an hour series," I said. In truth, I was sixty-five, but I thought I was done.

He said, "Just do the spinoff. Then you don't have to do anything."

I did, and then one movie of the week

turned into three movies of the week, and so on, and that went on for ten years. It wasn't a cool show, but I did push the fact that there was no violence and no bad language. And as I worked well into my seventies, I think I helped show that older folks are still employable. For that reason alone: **A**

2001

September 11. Terrorists attacked the United States in New York City, Washington DC, and Shanksville, Pennsylvania. It's one of those days that none of us will ever forget. I woke up, turned on the television, and saw the World Trade Center on fire. Like everyone else, I had trouble comprehending what I saw, especially when the second plane crashed into the building and then the towers fell . . . it was incredible in the sense that I didn't believe something like that could be real. It was like a movie. But it was real, and it brought back memories of the bombings of London in 1939 and the kamikaze pilots in World War II who were willing to die. The world is still feeling the impact of those attacks. **F**

2008

Barack Obama won the election for the forty-fourth president of the United States, becoming the country's first black president. I never ever thought I would see that in my lifetime. I thought I might see flying cars before I saw the first black president. But regardless of opinions about his performance, his election, like his campaign slogan, "Hope," made the future look much brighter. **A**

2014

Same-sex marriage became legal in about two-thirds of the country. By the end of the year thirty-five states allowed same-sex marriage, which I think is more than good — it's inevitable. I remember in the sixties and seventies, when people thought the institution was dead. I guess people were wrong. If one thing is clear from the dawn of human history, nothing is more powerful than love. Love is here to stay. **A**

Comments

Like every era of history, the years I have witnessed have been filled with all kinds of violence, prejudice, and stupidity, and yet every day someone is born who will discover a vaccine, invent new technology, write a song, find a peaceful way to battle injustice, conquer ignorance, and make a decision that will keep us human beings moving forward. How do I know? I have seen it happen. So as I think about a time when I will no longer be around to see what happens next, I have hope that future generations will continue to do better, to keep us moving in the direction where every generation will have the nourishment of hope.

LET'S HEAR IT FOR NEIGHBORLINESS

Recently Arlene and I went out to dinner in Beverly Hills and then saw Jane Lynch in her one-woman show. The next morning I realized I had lost my wallet. Here is the letter to the editor of our local newspaper I wrote a few days after my wallet mysteriously turned up in a neighbor's yard.

I moved to Malibu in 1986 when I was sixty-one years old. I'm closing in on ninety now. It's been a beautiful three decades, and I think it's time I expressed a little appreciation. As the years have piled on, some of my faculties began taking a hike: you know, misplacing the car key, my glasses, grocery lists — that sort of thing.

Once, I dropped my wallet on the sidewalk in front of the bank. Before I could miss it, a call came from the restaurant next door, Marmalade. Someone had dropped it off, knowing I go there a lot. I believe Ralph's Supermarket keeps a special drawer for the collection of credit cards I leave there on a regular basis, always neatly bound up in a rubber band.

Last week a good neighbor called to say she found my wallet in her front yard. How did it get over there? She didn't know. I don't know. None of us will ever know. But it got back to me.

Short of a nursing home, this neighborhood is the closest there is to assisted living I could get. Thanks to you all for looking after me so well.

When you get over the hill, I will do the same for you.

What a town!

The Dreams of an Old Man

This is really all about ordering a teepee. But you're going to have to wait before I get to that part.

When I was fourteen years old, Wendell Willkie came through Danville on a whistle-stop tour. The liberal Republican was drumming up support for his presidential run against FDR. My grandfather took me to the train station to hear him speak. This was a big event in our small town, and hundreds of people turned out. I had a hard time grasping his criticisms of the New Deal, but his notion of a One World government struck me as something novel. To a boy my age, that was a big wow!

We went home, and sometime later I saw my great-grandmother. She was a memorable character. As a young woman, one of her hands had been cut off in a thrasher, but that didn't stop her from doing anything. She raised a family, cooked, and knitted up a warehouse-worth of sweaters, scarves, and blankets. She was a hillbilly — tough stock. She sat on the back porch and smoked an old clay pipe and spouted off on things in a peculiar jargon. For instance, to her, junk food was "truck."

I can still hear her say, "Dickie, don't eat that truck."

Sitting in her chair, puffing on her pipe, she listened to me talk about Willkie and his One World idea, and then, when I finished, she widened her eyes, leaned forward, and, in her Southern Illinois accent, said, "When I was a little girl, long about your age, my dad took me to the train station to hear Abraham Lincoln. He was also running for president." Though we lived in the land of Lincoln, I could not imagine anyone, let alone my great-grandmother, having actually seen this American icon, the president who freed the slaves. I was impressed.

But not as impressed as I am today — a hundred and fifty years after Lincoln was assassinated in Ford's Theatre — knowing that my great-great-grandfather and great-grandmother listened to his speech and, in some minute, tangential manner, provided me with a direct link to that chapter in history. It is so long ago, almost unfathomably long ago, yet I can clearly remember the sound of my great-grandmother's voice as she said his name.

Over the years I have met my share of US presidents. Lyndon Johnson was the first. It was Columbus Day, and Julie Andrews and I were in a parade in San Francisco. We ended up at a lectern in Golden Gate Park, where Johnson was supposed to give a speech. But he was late; word came that he was stuck in Long Beach. "He's on his way," an official assured us, though he didn't know when the president would arrive.

As I stared out at the forty thousand people in the crowd, I saw an opportunity. I went to the microphone and pretended to give a campaign-type speech. "If I were president . . ." I then listed off the things I'd do: Get us out of Vietnam, promote civil rights, women's rights, environmental rights. . . . I was so far to the left that all I talked about was rights. As you can imagine, it went over big with that crowd.

Johnson eventually showed up with his hand wrapped in bandages. We were told his skin had been rubbed raw from shaking so many hands. After he spoke, I waited in line to present him a plaque from the Fellowship of Christians and Jews. Just ahead of me was a Boy Scout presenting another award. As they shook hands, Johnson spotted something out of the corner of his eye and suddenly said, "Goddamnit, I said no pictures!" He was reputed to be a salty curmudgeon, and apparently he really was.

I met Richard Nixon at a restaurant in Beverly Hills, and I shook hands with his more genial successor, Gerald Ford, at a fundraiser that was memorable for the waltz I did with his wife, Betty. At the time she was not yet sober. I don't know what she was taking or drinking, but she was on it. When we danced, I took hold of her with a vice-like grip and did not let go until the music ended. I was not going to lose the First Lady in front of all those people.

As unsteady as she was on her feet, her smile never wavered. Nor did her poise or pleasantness. I liked her. Her goodness and moral centeredness were apparent, despite the private demons she battled. Politically she was always on my side of issues like equal rights, abortion, and gun control. Personally she became an inspiration to me and many others when she got sober, following an intervention from her family. She was sixty years old at the time.

Four years later, in 1982, she founded the Betty Ford Center in Rancho Mirage, California. And in 1999, at age eighty-one, she was awarded the Congressional Gold Medal. Her candor, courage, and determination to help people transformed and saved countless lives, and she did much of that vital work in the senior years of her life. She kept moving.

Bill Clinton lived up to advance billing. He ignored me when we met in the Oval Office. Instead, he walked in, looked directly at Michelle, and said, "At last we meet." She was a tough one who had met everyone — and she melted. He gave her a hug and spoke only to her. I was wallpaper. He never even said hello to me, and Michelle was fine with that. So was I.

As many have noted, the man is the best speaker I've ever heard. FDR was a great orator and Reagan knew how to deliver a message, but Clinton had the ability to stand in front of any sized audience and speak to just one person.

Sometimes he did exactly that. After Carl Reiner received the Mark Twain Prize for American Humor in 2000, he and his wife, Estelle, spent the night in the Lincoln bedroom at the White House. At about 1 A.M. they heard a knock on the door. In walked Bill Clinton, wearing a sweatshirt. He sat and talked to them through the night about world issues, American history, anything Carl brought up. My friend was blown away. I would vote to reelect him again — I think he was that good at the job.

Obama, also impressive, drives me crazy. But I am a fan. I voted for him twice and thanked him once after he straightened my tie following a 2010 Fourth of July celebration in Washington, DC, where I performed with my a cappella group the Vantastix at Ford's Theatre. Which brings me back to Abraham Lincoln, a president who sits in a whole other realm from the others I have mentioned. My slender link to him resonates even more powerfully with me now, at age ninety. When I think about the future, my own and the years ahead that will not include me, I understand how intricately it is shaped by the past and how important it is to share the good things we had so we don't lose them.

I think this was a defining characteristic of my generation. We got through the Great Depression and pulled through World War II. We fought to defend the freedom others had died for in the past and to preserve it for future generations. We made tough decisions and learned and grew from them. I think we made the world a better place. Have subsequent generations done the same?

To me, the biggest deficiency today is trust. I would very much like to see trust make a comeback. I'll tell you something that made a lifelong impression on me. When I was a kid, in the middle of the Great Depression, there were a lot of homeless people on the street. "They aren't all bums," I remember hearing. "They're just down on their luck." People regularly knocked on our back door asking for food, which my mom always gave them. Everybody helped out if they could. I remember seeing a mark on the fence behind our house and others nearby. It meant that a softy lived in that house. Ours had a big X. Times were hard, and there was a sense that we all had to help each other get through it.

Trust was assumed where I grew up. Nobody ever thought about locking their door. On Saturday night, when we went to the movies, we simply walked out of the house. We left a light on, but otherwise the screen door slammed shut behind us, and that was it. You saw the same thing in houses on every block. When I was five years old, my mother would give me a nickel and send me on the streetcar four miles away to my grandparents' house. If something happened, she trusted that I'd be okay, that someone would help out.

I probably sound double my age when I go on about such things, an old man on a soapbox, but remembering the way people used to trust each other, along with other basic values, like kindness and manners, those are exactly the sorts of good things from the past we don't want to lose. Trust is not like a Norman Rockwell painting that people can see in a museum — once it's gone, it's hard to get it back.

I say this not as a warning but as an invitation to younger people. Talk to people my age. Don't let the gray hair, the brittle legs, or the long pauses between thoughts scare you. As stewards of the future, it's important to know the past was full of good stuff too — and to know what that was.

My great-grandparents' farm in southern Illinois comes to mind. Even my brother was born too late to know about it, but I went there a number of times. They had no electricity, no water — no anything. They had kerosene lamps for light and a pump in the kitchen for water. My great-grandfather got up at 4 A.M., ate steak and apple pie for breakfast, and then worked all day in the field. Their days were built around sustenance. They had an old pump organ in the living room that I banged on until they yelled at me to stop.

"We have to get up in the morning, Dickie! There's gonna be work to do."

Back then I thought it was incredible people could live that way; it's even more so now. There was something about the simplicity of that life that stands out to me as pure and perhaps more genuine than the clutter we drown in today. How much of what we have is essential to a good life? What is essential?

I might even ask: What is necessary to provide the best life going forward to future generations? Are we making those choices? Or are we erring on the side of commerce and clutter?

This has been on my mind since last Christmas when Arlene said she wanted a teepee for the backyard. (Yes, this is the aforementioned teepee part of this story — finally.) I said, "How about a nice necklace?" But I was joking — my wife doesn't wear jewelry. She's a creative person, like me, and her tastes are practical and playful, along the lines of dance lessons, arts and crafts materials, or even a new hula hoop. It's one of the things we have in common.

But a teepee?

Arlene explained that she had seen a kids-sized version in a catalog and thought it would it would be a fun novelty on the patio as the weather got warmer. "Rocky can hang out in there," she said.

Because this was a gift, I took the lead, did some research, and ordered a beautiful handmade teepee. Instead of the Boy Scout–sized tent we expected, the teepee that arrived measured sixteen feet tall and eighteen feet in diameter. The new addition now sits on a custom-built platform halfway up our backyard hill and fits into the landscape surprisingly well.

But that wasn't only half the surprise. Arriving with the teepee was a copy of a letter that Suquamish Indian leader Chief Seattle allegedly wrote to President Franklin Pierce in 1855 in response to the United States' determination to purchase the tribe's land. This popular and poetic homage to the environment begins, "The President in Washington sends word that he wishes to buy our land. But how can you buy or sell the sky? The land? The idea is strange to us. If we do not own the freshness of air and the sparkle of the water, how can you buy them?"

It goes on to ask even more profound and prophetic questions. "Your destiny is a mystery to us. What will happen when the buffalo are all slaughtered? The wild horses tamed? What will happen when the secret corners of the forest are heavy with the scent of many men and the view of the ripe hills is blotted with talking wires? Where will the thicket be? Gone! Where will the eagle be? Gone! And what is to say goodbye to the swift pony and then hunt? The end of living and the beginning of survival."

Interestingly, this oft-quoted letter did not prove to be authentic. In the course of researching its context, I learned a screenwriter had penned it in the 1970s, and its authenticity was simply assumed. But I found the real letter, the one that inspired the screenwriter, and it's equally powerful, if not more so due to the chief's anger and resignation that the white men didn't get it:

Your religion was written on the tables of stone by the iron finger of an angry God, so you would not forget it. The red man could never understand it or remember it. Our religion is in the ways of our forefathers, the dreams of our old men, sent them by the Great Spirit, and the visions of our sachems. And it is written in the hearts of our people.

Your dead forget you and the country of their birth as soon as they go beyond the grave and walk among the stars. They are quickly forgotten and they never return.

Our dead never forget this beautiful earth. It is their mother. They always remember and love her rivers, her great mountains, her valleys. They long for the living, who are lonely too and who long for the dead. And their spirits often return to visit and console us.

What are the dreams of this old man?

That we don't lose all the ways of our forefathers.

That younger generations realize we all are part of a continuum and act accordingly.

That young people talk to old people and hear their stories before they are gone.

That compassion becomes a priority, and cost is not a consideration.

That trust makes a comeback.

That young people watch Laurel and Hardy movies.

That they listen to Frank Sinatra records.

That they explore the pioneers of jazz.

That they appreciate the way Cary Grant dressed.

That people smile at strangers and say hello to each other more often than not.

That people of all ages cherish and revere the generosity and beauty of the earth as our home and mother and do everything they can to protect and preserve its health for future generations.

That someone writes a song about all this.

That the Vantastix record it. Soon.

That you order a teepee and see whether it doesn't make you think too.

Like everyone, I have my share of regrets, things I would do differently if given a chance. As I said, when I was a kid, the church organist noticed me playing, said I had talent, and offered to give me free piano lessons. But I only went twice. Mistake. Around that same time my mother signed me up for tap dance lessons. I got the chicken pox and never went back. Later those lessons would've come in handy.

As a teenager, I hung out with guys who started me smoking cigarettes. I wish I had never started. I didn't have the sense to quit until I was in my sixties. In my thirties, when I began to sing and dance, I should've taken singing and dancing lessons. I didn't. I was offered the lead in the movie *The Omen,* but I thought it was too dark, and the role went to Gregory Peck instead.

There are more, but there's only one regret on my list that I still have the ability to change, and I want to do it before it's too late. I was in fifth grade at Garfield Grade School. We were in class, and a friend of mine broke wind. The teacher smelled something funny and said, "Who lit a match in here?" No one raised a hand. The teacher got mad. They called each kid to the principal's office.

When it was my turn, I said, "It was Earl Copner."

I was going to also say, "He didn't light a match. He farted." But I didn't know how to say the word in front of the principal. I was embarrassed. I clammed up instead and left the poor guy hanging.

All these years later I want to finally say, "I'm sorry, Earl. It was my fault you got in trouble."

A Conversation with Carl

As I say frequently, I would not be where I am today without Carl Reiner. This Emmy-winning writer and actor, Oscar nominee, playwright, novelist, devoted husband, father, and proud grandfather is my long-time friend. He is also my mentor, a genius, and the smartest person I have ever known. Whenever I've needed advice, I have called Carl. Whenever I needed a clever line, I knew I could go to him and get a winner. And now, in need of another chapter for this book . . .

Seriously, given that Carl is three years older than me, I thought it would be interesting to speak with him about our relationship, about life, and about living a lot longer than either of us would have predicted. Luckily, he agreed. So one afternoon in April 2015 I went to his house in Beverly Hills, where we sat down in his office, a room filled with books, awards, and the interesting clutter amassed in one of Hollywood's great careers.

ME: So how is it being ninety-three?

CARL: Slower. (He smiles.) But hey, it's better than having stopped at ninety-two. How old are you?

ME: Eighty-nine.

CARL: How is that?

ME: A surprise.

CARL: I understand.

ME: We have known each other for about sixty years. Do you remember our first meeting?

CARL: I do — and I'll tell the whole story. I did a pilot called *Head of the Family,* a sitcom. I was starring in it, and I wrote thirteen episodes so that I would have a bible for other writers. I did the pilot with Barbara Britton, Sylvia Miles, and Morty Gunty in the other three parts. And it didn't sell. It was poor to failing. Horses and guns sold that year — no situation comedies. So I put it to bed.

However, I had thirteen episodes lying on my agent's desk. He was so upset because, as he said, the scripts were gold. He gave them to producer Sheldon Leonard, who wanted to try it again. But I said to Sheldon and my agent, "Fellows, I don't want to fail

243

twice with the same material."

Sheldon Leonard said, "You won't fail. We'll get a better actor to play you."

That better actor was you. Someone suggested you right away. I knew of you. I'd seen you on TV — the morning show you hosted when Walter Cronkite did the news for you. I went to see you in *Bye Bye Birdie,* and I was smitten. I went backstage to say hello, and that's where we met. I told you what I was planning, and as I recall, it was magic from that moment on.

ME: I had a pilot of my own that I wanted to do, something based on Jacques Tati's character Monsieur Hulot and set in Europe. But after reading your script, I threw my idea out the window. I had never read anything so good in my life.

CARL: It was one of those fortuitous moments. Everything fell into place, including Mary. That was another thing. I was looking for — well, I didn't know what I was looking for. Sheldon Leonard, in his infinite wisdom, said, "You'll know her when you see her." I saw about thirty girls, including Eileen Brennan, a very good actress. We flew her from New York and tested her. She was too ballsy and strong. Your character — not you but your character — couldn't have handled that. We told Sheldon she wasn't right.

We also told Danny Thomas, who'd picked up the check for the show, and he said, "What's that girl with the three names? She has good legs. She played on *Richard Diamond,* but all you saw were her legs. I brought her in to test for my daughter. But her nose went the wrong way."

We looked her up. It was Mary Tyler Moore. We called her, but she said she didn't particularly want to come in. She had gone to a couple of auditions and didn't make it. But she came anyway. As I recall, she walked in, I handed her the script and said, "Read the first scene." She read the first word and I sensed a ping in her voice. I made my hand into a claw, like the kind in an amusement arcade that picks up candy, and I walked across the room. She got scared.

I put my hand on top of her head and said, "Come with me." She had only said one word. Whatever it was, she said it perfectly. I walked her down the hall and said, "Sheldon, we found her." You were the only one who objected. She was twenty-three years old, and you were —

ME: I was twelve years older. I thought she was a little young.

CARL: I said, "My God, look at you together." Nobody ever asked if he was too old for her. They looked like a team from day one.

ME: I admired the way you ran the show. Your stuff was brilliant, but you never treated it as if it were written in stone. Everybody could contribute.

CARL: Luckily we had a creative cast. My agent suggested Rose Marie. He said, "Only one girl can play this. Rose Marie." And he was right. For the part of Buddy Sorrell, I was looking for a young guy like Mel Brooks. She said, "Morey Amsterdam. He's perfect."

I said, "The human joke machine?" I'd seen him at the little place he had on Broadway. He was the human joke machine, literally. He only needed two lines or even two words to make a joke; and he gave us a hundred thousand jokes. Having him in the room was one of the truly fortuitous things that happened.

ME: You purposely made it timeless — no slang, no reference to current events, nothing that would date it. What was your thinking behind that?

CARL: As soon as I saw the pilot, I knew it was a classy show. It was about a family. It was about my family. It was true, and I knew it would remain true a long time if we didn't put in anything that would date it.

ME: The show aired from 1961 to 1966 —

CARL: By the way, Dick, I've got to tell you something that will make you feel good. The show has been airing on one of the channels, and I have recorded them as they come on. Every once in a while I can't go to sleep, so I'll pop on a show, and I just laugh. I keep getting re-amazed by what you could do.

ME: And I am amazed by what you created. We did the show fifty-some years ago. It's aired practically nonstop. And while we've grown old in real life, on TV we haven't aged. We're stuck in our prime.

CARL: What's nice is that it's still on every night. I can't believe it. And the show is responsible for something nice that has happened now for three generations. It happened twenty years ago, it happened ten years ago, and it happened lately. Somebody comes up to me and says, "When I was a kid or eleven or twelve years old, I was funny. I knew I wasn't going to be a comedian, but I was funny. Then I saw *The Dick Van Dyke Show* and learned there's a thing called a writer. I could do that. I could be that Dick Van Dyke guy who writes for other people."

Over the years two or three dozen people must have said that to me.

ME: That's a tribute to your writing. Those shows do make it look fun.

CARL: It is fun. I write every day.

ME: But thanks to that show we are eternally young.

CARL: Scary.

ME: Actually it doesn't bother me. I'm just happy to be here.

CARL: A long time ago I was asked which theatrical project I am most proud of, and I answered, "Creating *The Dick Van Dyke Show,* hands down. I've done a lot of things, but that's one that informs my whole being."

ME: It's your life.

CARL: With a more talented person playing me.

ME: Neither of us has stopped working. Like me, you blew past age sixty-five, retirement age. Did you ever think of retirement?

CARL: Now, physically, I can't do very much. I did something at the TV Land Awards the other night, and it took a lot out of me. But I was very funny.

ME: Did you feel old at sixty-five?

CARL: I didn't give age a second thought. I was busy directing, producing, and acting.

If you're working, you don't think about it. You figure those milestones are just another day. In fact, I think somebody said I was eligible for Social Security. I said I didn't need it.

ME: Earlier in this book I have a chapter called "How Do You Know When You're Old?" When did you start to feel it?

CARL: I don't remember the exact moment. But it's when I look into the bathroom mirror in the morning and say, "Look who you are. What became of you?" There are all these spots and things. How could that be me?

ME: I remember when I turned eighty, I said, "This is old age? Fine. It's good with me." I didn't realize what was ahead.

CARL: Since turning ninety I've slowed down a lot. Every once in a while I will feel something and think my blood pressure just spurted. I will hear myself say, "This is it. I'm about to go." I have one salvation — a blood pressure cuff. I will put it on and check. It's anxiety. I'm ninety-three. How far can you go?

ME: I don't think about that.

CARL: I do — all the time. How am I going to go? Where am I going to be? What will I be doing? You know the line, "Is this the end of Rico?" Jimmy Cagney says that at the end of the movie *Little Caesar.* He's a gangster. He's on top of a water tower. They're shooting at him. His last words are, "Mother mercy, is this the end of Rico?" I think about it frequently: How am I going to go?

ME: I heard you in an interview say that you get up every morning, look at the obituaries, and if you're not there, you have breakfast.

CARL: I do that. Every morning. Looking, hoping I see a 101-year-old. Once in a while I do. When I see people in there that were eighty, seventy, and sixty, I think, "Oh, shit." The other day I saw a ninety-eight-year-old. That was good. There was hope.

ME: When you're writing, do you feel your age?

CARL: No, when I am writing and not thinking about my health, I could be fifty. I don't think about age. But other times I think I'm lucky; I still walk up and down the stairs. I walk up and down the block. Yesterday I forced myself to go around the block. At my age they tell you walking is the single most important thing you can do — after not dying, of course.

ME: I have been working out for years, but once I got into my seventies, I got a little curious: How much can I do? Now I work out as a matter of defiance. I still have vivid dreams of myself running across an open field, like a deer — that freedom.

CARL: That's a good dream. I dream all the time. I have to remember them because I go to a psychiatrist once a week and try to figure out what they're about.

ME: You're still in therapy?

CARL: Yeah. My wife found psychiatry when it was $15 an hour. She heard about it and said, "That's for me." Then we went together. Then I went alone. You realize there are things you can fix about yourself — or at least think about differently.

ME: After all these years, what are you still working on?

CARL: Anxiety.

ME: What is causing you anxiety?

CARL: Dying.

ME: In 1977 you directed George Burns in *Oh God.* He was famous for celebrating his age. Did he say anything you remember?

CARL: When the picture was over, I went backstage to say good-bye to him. I said, "George, you never talk about your family or anything. You always talk about vaudeville people." He said, "Family is boring. They're all boring." I said, "I'm fifty-five.

But you're eighty, and I always see pictures of you with two or three girls on your arm. What do I have to look forward to sexually when I get to be your age?" He said, "Carl, did you ever try to push an oyster into a slot machine?" That's a great line.

ME: What advice do you have for people in their fifties or sixties who are worried about getting old?

CARL: Find something that interests you, and stay with it. A good marriage is very healthy. I lucked out marrying what I call my LOML — my love of my life — and staying married for sixty-five years. People ask me how long I was married. I would explain I was married sixty-five years when Estelle died. But now I say, "She was married for sixty-five years. And in my head, I think she's still my wife. I'm not marrying anybody else. So I have been married seventy-two years now. I'm still married to her."

ME: I didn't expect to remarry or meet anyone new. I just fell in love.

CARL: Estelle was still singing when she was ninety-two. At sixty-three, she practiced in bed. Our daughter Annie filled in for her a year later when she was too sick to perform. But to the day she died, she had a ukulele in the bed with her. She made two albums with her uke, *Ukulele Mama 1* and *Ukulele Mama 2.* I bought her a very nice Martin uke. She said, "Why do I need such an expensive uke? You play it." Our son Lucas is now playing that uke.

ME: She loved to perform.

CARL: The last year of her life she had a lot of things wrong with her. But she was always there. In her head she was always fine. For the last year she couldn't get out of bed. As she got worse and worse, we had nurses all the time. Even when Mel [Brooks] came to visit, he'd come up for a few minutes and say hello. Then when she was really starting to go and had all her faculties about her, she spoke to each one of the kids separately. She apologized for not being a good mother, and they convinced her that she did her best. On the last day the hospice people were there. She was not breathing, at least that we could see. We talked to her, but she was not answering. Her eyes were not moving, her lids were down. Every once in a while we saw her take a breath, not much of a breath, but we saw it. The last hour of her life, there was no sound at all, nothing. We were just sitting there, and I said, "Let her go hearing herself sing." I got her album *Adult Songs for Children* and put on the song "Hey, You're Adorable." I said, "Play it up loud. Let her hear herself go out singing."

As it played, one of the nurses said, "She has such a lovely, sweet voice." Well, Lucas went up to his mother, who was just lying there, and he spoke loudly, right to her face, "Ma, one of the nurses say you have a lovely, sweet voice." She mouthed, "Thank you," and died.

ME: Just before Michelle died, she looked at me and said, "You made me a better person." Then she closed her eyes and —

CARL: The best way to go is to dream you're going and then go, in your sleep.

ME: Instead of talking about the end, let me ask you this: What has given your life the most meaning?

CARL: My kids being who they are. Every one of my kids, all three of them, turned out to be really good people, and that's the only thing you can take pride in, that you sent nontoxic people out into the world.

ME: I always thank my kids. I had no ambition or drive of any kind, and if it weren't for my kids, I would still be back in Danville, Illinois. But I had to get out and beat the bushes, and look what happened.

CARL: Pretty good.

ME: What advice do you have for younger people?

CARL: Be who you are. If you can, if you can afford to, do only things that please you.

ME: Unfortunately so many people don't like their jobs. They hate their work. If you love your work, it's like play.

CARL: That's right. If you can't do what you love in order to make a living, find a hobby that you can't wait to get to after work. You need passion and joy in your life. Family. Love. Passion. And joy.

THE THING THAT LASTS

The one thing that persists
from childhood through
whatever age you are right now
is the love we feel for one another
and still feel even more today.
Love is the thing that lasts.
You feel it more than the aches and pains.
You remember it when other memories
    fade.
You crave it when you have no taste
for anything else.
You pick it up when you feel weak.
It's on your smile in the morning
and in your dreams at night.
It's what you carry around with you every
    day.
It's what you take with you.
It's what you leave behind.
Love is the thing that lasts.
That makes it all worthwhile.
I wouldn't trade a minute of it.

A LIFE ACHIEVEMENT AWARD

At eighty-seven, I received a Life Achievement Award. It was presented to me at the annual Screen Actors Guild Awards gala. Carl Reiner was supposed to introduce me, but he came down with the flu, and Alec Baldwin stepped in at the last moment.

"I've been borrowing from Dick every time I step in front of the camera," he said. I doubt it — Alec is a gifted actor on his own, with more range than I ever had, but it was a nice thing to say, and that's what you do at those type of events: you say nice things.

I know because I introduced Julie Andrews when she received her Life Achievement Award, and a few years later I introduced my friend and TV wife, Mary Tyler Moore, and on both occasions I said very nice things. Of course, in the cases of both Julie and Mary, they were well deserved. There is not a bad word to say about either one of those women. When you think about it, that itself is worth an award these days, though, if you are like me, you are also thinking that should be the norm. Saying nice things is a good thing. Likewise, not saying bad things also works in your favor.

As for me, I barely knew what to say when I stepped onstage to accept my award. I looked out at the audience and saw George Clooney, Bryan Cranston, and Daniel Day-Lewis, among dozens of other stars in formals and tuxedos, right in front, giving me a standing ovation, and it threw off my concentration.

"Thank you, Mr. Lincoln," I said. "Such a thrill. That does an old man a lot of good." A montage of clips had preceded me on-stage (*The Dick Van Dyke Show, Diagnosis Murder, Mary Poppins, Chitty Chitty Bang Bang,* and *Bye Bye Birdie*), and I was honored my peers had decided to recognize my work, even if I was reluctant to describe it as work. "I've knocked around this business for seventy years, and I still haven't quite figured out what it is that I do," I said.

Backstage, in front of reporters, I made a candid admission. "If I don't have an audience, I am not very good," I said. "I need the audience to do their work."

It's true. And the work the audience does

is to laugh, clap, or applaud. Or sing. Or all of the above. The gift I have been given is the ability to make people feel good, and I can't begin to describe how that has made me feel. I understand why people commit to a life of service — nothing brings more joy than making someone else feel good.

My friend Julie Andrews said the same thing when she received her award. "I have so much joy in my work," she said, "and these days I've come to understand that the joy is all about the giving."

I found more truths and tips from previous recipients. Shirley Temple Black, for instance, said, "Start early." Betty White encouraged people to find a passion and pursue it. And Mary Tyler Moore told a story about ignoring advice that she should change her name if she hoped to get work. But as she said, she was Mary — Mary Moore. What would her father, George Tyler Moore, say if she changed her name?

"Then it hit me," she said. "Tyler was my middle name too. I was Mary Tyler Moore. I spoke it out loud. 'Mary Tyler Moore.' It sounded right. So I wrote it out on the form. And it looked right. It was right."

The lesson? Be real. Be honest. When I look back on a life deemed worthy of an award, I think my biggest achievement has been a body of work on and off screen that is positive. There aren't any black marks. And with that I am satisfied.

Early on in my Hollywood career I decided I wouldn't accept any parts that I would be embarrassed for my children to see, and that proved a good touchstone. Adhering to that strict sensibility cost me an opportunity to work with Cary Grant, who wanted me to work on one of his romantic comedies, which I thought was too risqué. Now, looking back, the stuff I thought risqué is laughingly benign, more clever than crude. But it was the early sixties — what did I know?

And that's the thing. When you are living life, it is impossible to know what will happen. You take your best shot; you make your best guess. My brother, for instance, was the number-one choice to play Gilligan on the TV classic *Gilligan's Island.* But he turned it down. He feared, perhaps rightly, that he would be typecast forever as Gilligan and never have the long, varied career he envisioned.

A year later he was offered the lead on a sitcom called *My Mother the Car.* Before he took it, he asked what I thought. I said a show about a car that talked didn't seem like a strong idea. Then Jerry asked what I was working on. I said I was about to go to Europe to make a movie.

"What's it about?" he asked.

"A car that flies," I said.

So you never know. I never would have guessed that I would meet idols of mine such as Stan Laurel, Buster Keaton, Cary Grant, Gene Kelly (we were actually in a movie together, *What a Way to Go*), and Fred Astaire, who floored me when he said in a radio interview, "I like the way Van Dyke moves." (I heard that while I was in the car and nearly drove off the road.)

I remember bumping into Fred Astaire when he was in his early eighties, younger than I am now but still up there. "Do you still dance?" I asked.

"Yes," he said. "But it hurts now."

That might be the best summation I have heard of old age. You do the same things you always did — or try to — except that it hurts. You continue to move. It just takes longer. It may also require more persuasion than was needed in the past. It may also require Advil before or after. It ain't easy. No one said it would be — and it isn't. But what are you going to do? This is what we have, this life of ours.

If it were up to me, more people would get life achievement awards for the choices they have made. Somehow we entertainers seem to have locked up this honor. I have lost track of all the award shows where Hollywood gives life achievement awards just for going to work and doing our job. I am not complaining or criticizing, but there is a long list of those who do the same thing and don't get the accolades. Teachers. Doctors. Inventors. Nurses. Parents who ensure that their child will be the first in their family to get a college education. Volunteers. People who hold sick babies in the hospital. The list goes on.

Life is a roll of the dice. You do your best. My résumé includes booze and cigarettes. I had a drinking problem, and I was a long-time smoker. I had trouble breaking both of those bad habits. I wish I had never started down the path with either one. But I don't look at them as black marks on my record; in fact, I see quitting them as an accomplishment and, no doubt, contributing factors to why I am still here. And being here, after all, is the point.

Well, part of the point. The other part is making it count, making sure you cover all the bases. And what are those bases? Let's start with the big stuff. Should you believe in a higher power or not? I say yes. But I don't believe in a higher power that is owned by any one religion or one that shows a preference to gender or color. I don't believe in a him or her, a he or she, or the god claimed by a specific religion. I believe in a higher power that we have to answer to. My higher power has something to do with the inexplicable, massiveness, mystery, and beauty of the universe.

The higher power I believe in does not discriminate and does not tolerate discrimination. The higher power I believe in has left it up to us to figure out how to navigate all the complexities that get in the way of us understanding that the only things that truly matter are compassion and love. We get the gift of life; we have to figure out how to make it matter.

I also believe in the power of prayer. I don't know if prayer is a pipeline to a higher power, but I remember being a young TV host in New Orleans where, despite big local ratings, I felt confused and frightened about my prospects for the future, and I prayed for a break. I am not talking a one-time deal; I didn't leave a message on a spiritual answering machine: "Hey, it's Dick Van Dyke in New Orleans, and I can't raise a family on $10,000 a year. Help!" I prayed several times a day. I was serious. I wanted direction, a path toward more stability and security.

"Something has got to happen," I said to myself. And then it did. Out of the blue Byron Paul, an old Air Force buddy, got me an audition at CBS in New York. After my audition they gave me a seven-year contract for double the money I'd been making. I was speechless.

"Speaking on behalf of Dick, he accepts," Byron said. "He is thrilled."

Answered prayers? Or just luck? I don't know. Both work. I don't see a need to sweat the difference. But from what I have seen, prayer has a power of its own. Prayer is a way we talk to ourselves, and I think that creates a sense of clarity, strength, and confidence that opens the door to change.

It was like that with my drinking. For years I tried treatment programs, rehab, and AA meetings without being able to stay sober. Then I tried prayer. I would say, "Please take this away from me. Please remove the power this has over me."

Gradually the booze started losing its effect. Instead of feeling happy and relaxed, I got a little dizzy and headachy, and then the urge just fell away. I never wanted to drink again — and I didn't.

Is that proof of anything? Only that prayer worked for me. It still does.

The thing you know when you get up around my age is that there are no rules, no signposts you must hit to get where you are going. In fact, the not-so-secret secret is that no one knows where they're going — or where they'll end up. You don't arrive as much as you run out of gas or break down.

Actually, as I think about it, the only rules are the rules of the road, and we really need to follow them if the younger generations are going to have half a chance of living as long as me and enjoying their old age half as much.

Wait your turn.
Follow the speed limit.
Signal before changing lanes.
Stop at red lights and stop signs.
Be courteous and let the other guy in.
Don't take up more than your share of the road.
Don't drive drunk.
Pay attention to what you're doing — stop looking at your phone.
Carpooling is good.
Wave if you see someone you know.
Don't cut anyone off. It doesn't make you get there any faster — and no one likes a cutter.
Don't honk if there is traffic or get frus-

trated if you get lost. Eventually you get where you were supposed to end up. It may not be where you intended to go, but it all works out in the end.

Singing in the car remedies any kind of road rage.

One thing I know for sure, something that is common knowledge to everyone who gets up in years enough to be considered old or, more specifically, around and beyond the average lifespan (as I said earlier — and it's worth repeating — men and women turning sixty-five today can expect, on average, to reach their mideighties, according to the Social Security Administration): the end is coming, and coming sooner rather than later. (It speeds up too.) None of us knows what that will be like other than it will be the end. As in: fade to black. THE END.

The obvious question is: Do I think about it? My answer is yes, I do — but no more than I ever did, which hasn't ever been that often. I have never been plagued by the kind of neuroses that cause others to constantly check for lumps or fear that each new pain is a white flag signaling that they are on their final lap. I have what I would call the enviable ability to focus on whatever I am doing, without worrying about what hap-

pened before or what might — or might not
— happen next.

What eats people up is anxiety. It creates
the tyranny of the "should haves" — I
should have done this. I should have done
that. My advice: do what you can, try your
best, and then don't worry about it.

One last note: I hope I don't come off in
this book as thinking I know everything — I
don't. I don't claim to know much of
anything unless it involves lyrics and a tune.
But I do know this:

If you are young, get used to having old
people around. There's only going to be
more of us — including you!

If you are middle-aged, don't think about
getting old.

If you are already old, congratulations,
you now know what I know! There is no
finish line. Stay open to whatever happens.
Don't be scared of dying. Be more frightened that you haven't finished living. Make
living a life achievement.

Keep moving.

Or, as the kids say, #KeepMoving.

ACKNOWLEDGMENTS

Here we are, at the conclusion of this book. For those who didn't close it a page earlier — and even for those who did — thank you for purchasing this book and spending time with me. I hope you enjoyed it and go on your way with a smile, a spring in your step, and some positive thoughts about aging. Remember, if nothing else, *keep moving* — and help other people do the same. We're all in this together.

To that point, I want to thank all the people who helped make the stories and events I wrote about possible, starting with my parents (good genes cannot be underestimated); my extended family of grandparents, aunts, and uncles; my brother, Jerry, who provided some very funny lines; my immediate family of my children, grandchildren, and great-grandchildren; and my friends and colleagues with whom I've worked over the years, as I frequently think about the projects we worked on together and treasure the memories.

As I said in my 2012 memoir, I have lived a lucky life in and out of show business, lucky in so many ways, not the least of which is making it to eighty-nine years old in good health and with a sound mind, my sense of humor still intact, and someone special I wake up in the morning and look forward to spending the day with. This book would not have been possible without my wife, Arlene. Throughout the writing process she recalled stories, provided details, double-checked dates, rounded up photos, worked on corrections, and kept the writers writing. At each work session she also made sure we had plenty of hot coffee and fresh laughter.

Likewise, this book would not exist without Jeff Kolodny, my manager at Paradigm, and Dan Strone, my agent at Trident Media Group, who believed in and then convinced me that I had something to say on the subject of aging. At the outset I feared this would be a very short book, inasmuch as I thought I only had two words to say on the subject — "Keep moving" — a pretty short book if you ask me. Fortunately I was wrong and Jeff and Dan were right. So thank you to both of them. Also, as I sit here at my dining room table, I am applauding Jackie Triggs and Chelsea Grogin, who obtained the permissions that made it possible for us to use the photos in this book, and I extend a note — no, make that enough notes — for an entire song of appreciation to Amanda Murray, my editor at Weinstein Books, and her team, Patricia Mulcahy and Christine Marra. I turned a manuscript over to them, and they turned it into a book. As a lifelong fan of magic tricks, I think that's a pretty good one.

And speaking of magic, I want to thank Todd Gold, my cowriter on this, our second book together, who spent the first six months of the year showing up at my house in the afternoon for a three o'clock cup of coffee. As we sat at the dining room table where I am now, he would laughingly assure me that our wide-ranging conversations would result in a book — and not just any old book, but one that people would enjoy reading. I had my doubts. My brother even stared him down one day and flat-out said, "What are you going to say? Everything about the subject has already been written." Todd was not phased. "Let's keep moving," he said. "Let's see what happens." Lo and behold, this happened.

And now I'm going to see if my wife wants

to go out to dinner.

Oh, one last reminder: never go down the stairs sideways.

ABOUT THE AUTHOR

Dick Van Dyke is a Hollywood icon and *New York Times* bestselling author of *My Lucky Life In and Out of Show Business*. He has received the Theatre World Award, a Tony, a Grammy, and four Emmy awards, as well as the Screen Actors Guild Life Achievement Award in 2013. He lives in California. **Todd Gold** is a *New York Times* best-selling author who has collaborated on several dozen books with celebrities including Dick Van Dyke, Belinda Carlisle, Maureen McCormick, Drew Barrymore, and Sonny Bono, among others. He is currently the Executive Editor of XFINITY TV.

The employees of Thorndike Press hope you have enjoyed this Large Print book. All our Thorndike, Wheeler, and Kennebec Large Print titles are designed for easy reading, and all our books are made to last. Other Thorndike Press Large Print books are available at your library, through selected bookstores, or directly from us.

For information about titles, please call:
(800) 223-1244

or visit our Web site at:
http://gale.cengage.com/thorndike

To share your comments, please write:
Publisher
Thorndike Press
10 Water St., Suite 310
Waterville, ME 04901